Cambridge Elements

Elements in Current Archaeological Tools and Techniques
edited by
Hans Barnard
Cotsen Institute of Archaeology
Willeke Wendrich
Polytechnic University of Turin

RETROSPECTIVE AND PROSPECTIVE FOR SCIENTIFIC PROVENANCE STUDIES IN ARCHAEOLOGY

A.M. Pollard
University of Oxford

Shaftesbury Road, Cambridge CB2 8EA, United Kingdom

One Liberty Plaza, 20th Floor, New York, NY 10006, USA

477 Williamstown Road, Port Melbourne, VIC 3207, Australia

314–321, 3rd Floor, Plot 3, Splendor Forum, Jasola District Centre, New Delhi – 110025, India

103 Penang Road, #05–06/07, Visioncrest Commercial, Singapore 238467

Cambridge University Press is part of Cambridge University Press & Assessment, a department of the University of Cambridge.

We share the University's mission to contribute to society through the pursuit of education, learning and research at the highest international levels of excellence.

www.cambridge.org
Information on this title: www.cambridge.org/9781009592192

DOI: 10.1017/9781009592208

When citing this work, please include a reference to the DOI 10.1017/9781009592208

First published 2025

A catalogue record for this publication is available from the British Library

ISBN 978-1-009-59219-2 Hardback
ISBN 978-1-009-59222-2 Paperback
ISSN 2632-7031 (online)
ISSN 2632-7023 (print)

Retrospective and Prospective for Scientific Provenance Studies in Archaeology

Elements in Current Archaeological Tools and Techniques

DOI: 10.1017/9781009592208

First published online: January 2025

A.M. Pollard
University of Oxford

Author for correspondence: Mark Pollard, mark.pollard@arch.ox.ac.uk

Abstract: Provenance has been one of the major scientific applications in archaeology for a hundred years. The 'golden age' began in the 1950s, when large programmes were initiated focussing on bronzes, ceramics, and lithics. However, these had varying impact, ranging from wide acceptance to outright rejection. This Element reviews some of these programmes, mainly in Eurasia and North America, focussing on how the complexity of the material, and the effects of human behaviour, can impact on such studies. The conclusion is that provenance studies of lithic materials and obsidian are likely to be reliable, but those on ceramics and metals are increasingly complicated, especially in the light of mixing and recycling. An alternative is suggested, which focusses more on using scientific studies to understand the relationship between human selectivity and processing and the wider resources available, rather than on the simple question of 'where does this object come from'.

Keywords: provenance, archaeological theory, resource-scape, human resource selection, human materials processing

ISBNs: 9781009592192 (HB), 9781009592222 (PB), 9781009592208 (OC)
ISSNs: 2632-7031 (online), 2632-7023 (print)

Contents

At the 1928 meeting of the British Association for the Advancement of Science in Glasgow, the 'Sumerian Committee' of the BAAS made its first report, including the analysis of 34 bronze objects (Desch, 1929). The Committee, constituted of leading British archaeologists and metallurgists, was established to 'report on the probable source of the supply of copper used by the Sumerians'. Thus was born one of the first interdisciplinary projects carrying out the chemical analysis of archaeological copper alloy objects, with the express aim of provenance. Nearly 100 years later, it is perhaps time to reflect on such activity.

This Element seeks to chart the development, degrees of success, and suggests a possible re-focussing for one of the major activities in scientific archaeology – the use of chemical and isotopic measurements on archaeological artefacts to determine the origin of the raw materials used to make these objects, commonly referred to as provenance studies. The focus here is on inorganic materials, particularly copper alloys, ceramics, and lithic materials, since several hundred thousand analyses have been published on these categories; numerically, studies on other materials generally pale into insignificance. Organic materials, particularly amber, have been historically important, and others, such as textiles, the production and trade of which have been key economic activities, are under-represented in the provenance literature because of poor survival and also the need for more specialized analytical techniques such as proteomics and light stable isotope ratios.

Inorganic provenance studies were widely adopted from the 1960s onwards because in principle they can elucidate trade and exchange patterns in the ancient world, and, therefore, contribute to studies of contact between societies, either in terms of trade in materials or other forms of social transfer of goods. Perhaps even more significantly, it can provide proxy evidence for the exchange of ideas. The rise of provenance was facilitated by two parallel developments – the increasing availability of instrumental methods of chemical analysis, and changing theoretical concepts of the role of material culture within archaeology. The growing scepticism in some quarters towards provenance studies from the 1980s onwards was partly the consequence of a gradually increasing recognition of the complexity of the production processes for all but the simplest of artefacts, including a growing appreciation of the potential for recycling in some materials, particularly glass and metals. However, rather than signalling the end of materials analysis as a tool for provenance studies, these potentially confounding features can present interesting new challenges and unexpected opportunities for the modern archaeologist. In fact, they transform the concept of provenance from the apparently simple question of 'where does this object come from?' to the much more interesting one of 'how did humans manage and use the raw materials at their disposal to produce these artefacts?' Given that the ultimate aim of archaeology is to understand past human societies, this seems to provide a very fruitful and important avenue for future research.

1 The Provenance Hypothesis

Provenance in this context means identification of the source of the raw materials used to make archaeological objects. For ceramics, this corresponds to the source of the clay used, and perhaps the temper added. For copper alloys, it can be interpreted as the mine from which the copper ores are extracted, but it might involve multiple mines if alloying metals (tin, zinc) are added. Archaeologically, the term can be extrapolated from the direct identification of source to include the matching of a set of artefacts (the unknown group) with another set (the control group), the *implication* being that they come from the same place, without necessarily identifying the specific geological source(s). The former exercise can be considered as *provenance-to-source*, and the second *provenance-to-match*. This definition is very different to that used in art history, where provenance means the lifehistory (biography) of the artefact, ideally documenting the sequence of all owners (and hence locations) of a particular work of art since its creation. Some authors, particularly in the USA (e.g., Price and Burton, 2011: 213), have promoted the use of the term *provenience* to define the 'birthplace' of the object, and *provenance* to signify the 'resume' (biography) of the object. Although this is an important distinction, and embraces the art historical definition, the majority of archaeologists simply use the term *provenance* to cover both of these definitions, perhaps taking the view that 'birthplace' is part of 'biography'.

It is important to emphasize that 'provenance-to-match' has a much longer history in archaeology than scientific provenance studies. Similarities in material culture rapidly became one of the key markers for defining cultural groupings, and particular forms of ceramics, such as Roman transport amphorae, or red-gloss Samian ware, arranged into intricate typologies, have been key indicators of trade and exchange across the empire from Spain to India. These parallels are deduced from visual study of form – careful classification of shape, manufacturing details, and decorative features – often supplemented by visual examination of fabric – the colour and texture of the ceramic paste. Thus, the framework for studying provenance was already in place when Weigand *et al.* (1977) observed that 'in many instances there will exist differences in chemical composition between pottery from different sources that will exceed, in some recognizable way, the differences observed within pottery from a given source'. They termed this the 'provenience postulate', and suggested that it was the basis of all studies involving provenance attribution using chemical analysis. In 2001, Wilson and Pollard (2001: 507–508) attempted to clarify and systematize the assumptions behind the scientific provenance of archaeological materials by setting out six criteria for the 'provenance hypothesis':

i) The prime requirement is that some chemical (or isotopic) characteristic of the geological raw material(s) is carried through (unchanged, or predictably relatable) into the finished object.
ii) That this 'fingerprint' varies between potential geological sources available in the past, and that this variation can be related to the geographical (as opposed to perhaps a broad depositional environment) occurrences of the raw material. *Inter*-source variation must be greater than *intra*-source variation for successful source discrimination.
iii) That such characteristic 'fingerprints' can be measured with sufficient precision in the finished artefacts to enable discrimination between competing potential sources.
iv) That no 'mixing' of raw materials occurs (either before or during processing, or as a result of re-cycling of material), or that any such mixing can be adequately accounted for.
v) That post-depositional processes either have no effect on the characteristic fingerprint or that such alteration can either be detected (and the altered elements or sample be discounted) or that some satisfactory allowance can be made.
vi) That any observed patterns of trade or exchange of finished materials are interpretable in terms of human behaviour. This presupposes that the outcome of a scientific provenance study can be interfaced with an existing appropriate socio-economic model, so that such results do not exist *in vacuo*.

The first requirement reflects the idea of the 'fingerprint' – a characteristic element, set of elements, or isotopic composition which passes through from the source material to the object, ideally with no change. The possibility of a quantifiable change to the fingerprint through the various steps of the processing (depending on material) has to be acknowledged, but presents significant challenges in reality – it would require considerable supporting evidence to conclude that the difference observed in the fingerprint between source and product is due to processing (e.g., volatilization of certain elements at high temperatures) rather than signifying something else. The crux of the hypothesis is captured in points (ii) and (iii), particularly if the aim is provenance to source. Different geological sources (of ore, clay or rock, and so on) can only be distinguished if the fingerprint varies between alternative sources, if the internal variation in the fingerprint is less than that between sources, and the measurement technology is capable of measuring these differences. It also relies on the assumption that sources are geographically discrete. It might be of limited use archaeologically if a geological source of clay consists of a large chemically homogeneous river valley or flood plain (e.g., the Nile, or the Indus), rather than specifically located clay deposits (although it might be the case that what appears to be a chemically homogeneous deposit using one set of indicators (e.g., major elements) might show significant trends when a different set (e.g., trace elements) is used). Point (v) requires that what is measured as a fingerprint is (ideally) unaffected by post-depositional factors such as selective corrosion or contamination from groundwater.

Point (iv) – no mixing or recycling – is perhaps the issue that has dominated theoretical discussions of provenance. It is self-evident that, at least for provenance-to-source, any mixing of material from sources with different fingerprints will make it more difficult to assign an object to a specific source. Depending on the number of potential sources involved, and the magnitude of diversion in the measured fingerprint, it could simply result in less confidence in the assignment of object to source, or it could give rise to the creation of an entirely 'fictitious source' – the mixture resulting in data which, when plotted on an appropriate graph, appear to form a coherent source group, but which do not actually correspond to any real source. This is a case where provenance-to-match has a distinct advantage – if the characteristics of the unknown objects match those in the control material, then a common source can be proposed, even if it is itself unknown. The issue of mixing and recycling is discussed further next.

The final point was effectively a plea to interpret the results of any provenance study in terms of real human behaviour, rather than relying on abstract arrows on maps showing the movement of objects, apparently without the aid of human intervention. Trivially, this might involve thinking about how objects can move – as trade, gifts, tribute, war booty, and so on – and also about the mode of transport – maritime, riverine, or land. However, we must avoid the trap of assuming that human activities in the past carried the same meaning as they do today. Uniformitarianism is not a reliable guide in archaeology. Trade and exchange do not necessarily reflect purely commercial activities or 'market forces'. Marcel Mauss (1872–1950) showed how in many societies gift exchange was at the heart of creating and maintaining relationships both within and between social groupings (Mauss, 1923–1924). Karl Polyani (1886–1964) proposed that there were three modes of exchange: reciprocity, redistribution, and market exchange (Polyani, 1944), although not necessarily mutually exclusive. Gift exchange is a form of reciprocity; redistribution implies some centralized control of distribution, often via a central depot, and market

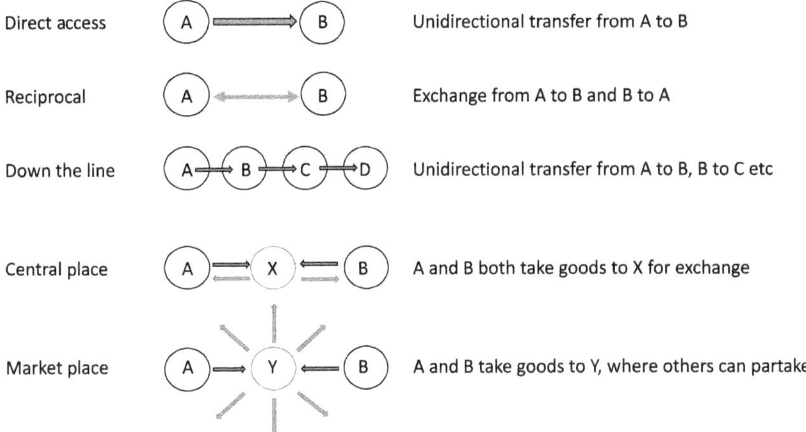

Figure 1 Some simple models of trade and exchange, redrawn from Renfrew and Bahn (2020: 371)

exchange involves a specific central location, but not necessarily a financial transaction. The particular mode of exchange is clearly linked with considerations of scale and organization – trading is very different in the context of a centralized imperial economy such as China or Rome, compared with differently regulated trading between independent tribal groups, or between traders working across the borders of settled sedentary populations and nomadic pastoralists. Renfrew and Bahn (2020: 371) have combined these social and economic considerations with various forms of settlement organization to produce a series of models for the exchange of physical commodities, some of which are redrawn in Figure 1. These range from direct contact between A and B to intermediate markets (A to market, market to B) to down-the-line trade (A to B to C to D, and so on). The form of exchange has an important influence on the distribution of particular objects, and also on how we should interpret provenance – as discussed in Section 7.1, in down-the-line trade, time taken to travel could be a factor in understanding the significance of finding objects from A at site D.

2 The Origins of Chemical Analysis in Archaeology

All of the examples discussed in this Element are predicated on the chemical analysis of inorganic objects. This application of the art of chemical analysis to archaeological artefacts has a long prehistory. The traditional methods of assay for gold – by separating the gold from silver by fire, or using the touchstone – have been known since at least the 2nd millennium BCE (Pollard, 2016). It is undoubtedly the case that miners and metalworkers were able to assay ores and precious metals long before the advent of analytical chemistry, and, indeed, the need for such assay provided an impetus for the development of chemistry (Greenaway, 1962, 1964). Cuneiform tablets from Mesopotamia (from the early 2nd millennium BC) describe the quantitative assay of gold by fire (Levey, 1959). For example, one 1st millennium BCE text says '2 minas 2 shekels of gold were put into the furnace, 10 1/2 shekels of them were lost in the furnace, 1 mina 51 1/2 shekels of dark gold came out of the furnace' (Levey, 1959: 33). Since 60 shekels = 1 mina, we can calculate that the original purity of this gold was around 91.4%. The Medieval Arab scholar Geber (Abu Mūsā Jābir ibn Hayyān, c. 721–c. 815 CE) shows a knowledge of the purification of gold, referring to gold 'sustaining the Tryal of the cupel, and cement' (Holmyard, 1928: 63), and his works were translated into English by Richard Russel in 1678. From at least the late 13th century CE, the Royal Mint (established within the Tower of London around 1279 CE) has routinely assayed the fineness of English gold and silver coinage (Watson, 1962). The gold coinage of Henry III was certified as 'fine' (i.e., 24 carat, or 100% gold) in 1257 CE, and Edward III established a gold currency at 99.48% purity in 1343. This declined over the next two centuries, until the 'Great Debasement' of Henry VIII when it declined to 83.33%, to be reinstated to 99.45% by Edward VI in 1550. Such evidence comes from the results of an ancient ceremony known as the 'Trial of the Pyx' carried out at the Mint since the late 13th century, in which the *Miles Argentarius* (Assay Master) certifies the fineness of the coinage, the method of which is 'differing but little from the modern fire-assay of silver' (Watson, 1962: 6). Hence, the assay of precious metal precedes modern chemical analysis by many centuries.

Many surviving medieval European texts give increasingly clear descriptions of the process of precious metal purification, and also for assaying base metal ores. Theophilus' *On Divers Arts*, written c. 1110–1140 CE, probably by the Benedictine monk Roger of Helmarshausen in Hesse, central Germany (Hawthorne and Smith, 1963), describes in Book III (Chapter 23) how to refine silver in a porous ash-lined cupel, using added lead to promote the oxidation of impurities. He also describes (Chapter 33) how to cement gold in order to purify it using a process which involves creating a 'sandwich' of thin sheets of gold alternating with layers of a mixture of recycled ground ceramics or burnt clay (two-thirds) with common salt (one-third) moistened with urine, heated in a fire-tested 'casserole dish'. Heating the casserole for 24 hours causes the salt to remove impurities, and, after a number of repetitions of the process, pure gold is obtained. The fineness of the original gold can be established by comparing the weight of the refined gold with that of the original. Further chapters (69 and 70) describe how to separate gold from copper in gilded scrap metal by cupellation in a bone-ash crucible, and how to separate gold from scrap gilded silver by heating with sulfur, which allows both gold and silver to be recovered.

The first European book to give a very clear description of assaying is the *Probierbüchlein*, possibly first published in Germany in 1518, although Annaliese Sisco and Cyril Stanley Smith (1949), the translators of this text into English, believe that the first edition is that of 1534 printed in Maydeburg. It was produced in numerous editions through the 16th and 17th centuries, and contained clear practical instructions for the purification of gold and silver by cementation, but also procedures for dissolving metals and ores in mineral acids for parting or assay, much as is still done today. It was the main source of such information in Europe until Lazarus Ercker's *Beschreibung allerfürnemisten mineralischen Ertzt und Berckwercksarten* (1574) (Sisco and Smith, 1951), which provided the first widely available European textbook for miners on assaying ores. This was extensively translated across Europe, including an English version published by Sir John Pettus (1683) as *Fleta Minor, or, the Laws of Art and Nature in Knowing, Judging, Assaying, Fining, Refining and Inlarging the Bodies of Confined Metals*. According to Pettus' translation, Ercker's introduction says:

> 'To learn and understand the way of Assaying, Proving and Refining of Metals, is an Excellent, Noble science, and an Antient and profitable Art, long since found out by the Art of Alchimy and Chimistry, as also all other Works of the Fire, by which not only the nature of Oars and Mines, and what Metalls contained in them are known; . . .'.

Clearly, the arts of assay were well-known long before analytical chemistry, and also that these methods all involved trial by fire – essentially a smaller-scale version of the processes required to reduce metals from their ores, or separate gold from silver, and therefore requiring access to metallurgical furnaces and facilities. It was not until the late 18th century CE that a different method emerged in Europe, ultimately giving rise to quantitative gravimetric analytical chemistry. This consisted of precipitating a known compound of a particular element out of a solution created by dissolving the sample in a suitable solvent. By employing a sequence of specific precipitations, a series of different elements can be quantified from the same solution. By weighing the amount of sample dissolved, and weighing the dried precipitate(s), the proportion of the precipitated element in the sample can be calculated, providing allowance can be made for the form in which the element is precipitated – for example, if tin (Sn) is precipitated as tin oxide (SnO_2), it would require correction by a factor of $(119/(119+2\times16))$, or 0.79, to reflect the proportion of oxygen in the compound. This could not have been calculated in this way until the atomic weights of the elements had been established, which began with John Dalton's '*New System of Chemical Philosophy*' (Dalton, 1808; 1827). Before that, an empirical observation would have been made (by fire) to calculate the proportion of metallic tin in the oxide precipitate.

Thus, at least in the chemical laboratory, trial by fire gradually gave way to gravimetric analysis, originally known as the 'humid method'. The first systematic exposition was that of Torbern Bergman (1735–1784) at the University of Uppsala, Sweden, who published a protocol for the aqueous gravimetric analysis of gemstones entitled '*Disquisitio chemica de terra gemmarum*' (Bergman, 1777). The big advance here was the use of an alkali fusion to bring the gemstone into solution, but Bergman's precipitation protocol was not very rigorous, and was subsequently improved by Martin Heinrich Klaproth (1743–1817) in Berlin (Klaproth, 1792/3) and Nicolas-Louis Vauquelin (1763–1829) in Paris (Vauquelin, 1799). These three analytical protocols have been re-published and compared by Oldroyd (1973).

The earliest report of the quantitative gravimetric chemical analysis of a metal appears to be that of Gustav von Engeström (1738–1813), who published a paper in 1776 on the composition of the imported white copper alloy paktong from China, which he found to contain approximately 29% nickel (with some cobalt). A year previously, von Engeström (1775) had published an analysis of imported zinc oxide from China, thus showing that he was engaged in understanding the nature of these imports – 'industrial espionage' to allow Europe to compete with Chinese technology. Bergmann himself published '*Dissertatio Chemica de Analysi Ferri*' in 1781. Given these dates for the early chemical analyses of metals in the late 1770s, it is remarkable to note that the earliest published chemical analyses of archaeological metal artefacts can be traced to 1777 by Johann Christian Wiegleb (1732–1800), read to the Kurmainzische Akademie Nutzlicher Wissenschaften, Mainz, on 2 April 1777 (Wiegleb, 1777; Pollard, 2018). He used nitric acid to dissolve the metal, but only measured tin, and assumed that the rest was copper. A few years later, Michel Jean Jérome Dizé (1764–1852) published the tin content of five Roman, one Greek, and two Gallic copper alloy coins (Dizé, 1790). Klaproth, in his better-known publication dated to 1792/3 (but actually read to the Royal Academy of Sciences and Belles-Lettres of Berlin on 9 July 1795, and published in 1798), reported the chemical analyses of six Greek and nine Roman coins, measuring directly copper, lead, and tin, and, in some samples, iron and silver – thus providing the earliest realistic analyses of ancient coins, justifiably earning him the title of the first archaeological chemist (Caley, 1949; Pollard, 2016), in addition to his renown as a mineral chemist.

3 The First Expressions of Provenance

Within a few decades of these first chemical analyses of archaeological objects in the late 18th century, the idea soon began to emerge that the chemical characteristics of exotic objects – those deemed not to be local to the point of recovery – might give some indication of where they had come from. The first such explicit observation was that of Karl Christian Traugott Friedeman Göbel (1794–1851), Professor of Chemistry and Pharmacy at Dorpat, Estonia, from 1828. His volume (Göbel, 1842) entitled '*Ueber den Einfluss der Chemie auf die Ermittelung der Völker der Vorzeit oder Resultate der chemischen Untersuchung metallischer Alterthümer insbesondere der in den Ostseegouvernements vorkommenden, Behufs der Ermittelung der Völker, van welchen sie abstammen*' was a landmark publication in many ways. The title ('About the influence of chemistry on the determination of the peoples of the past, or results of the chemical analysis of metallic antiquities') for the first time explicitly linked the chemistry of metallic antiquities to the 'determination of the peoples of the past'. It was also the largest compilation of archaeological bronze analyses up to that date (119), of which 55 were his own (recording copper, tin, zinc and lead) and the remainder were from other analysts, including 32 re-published from Klaproth. In his introduction, he articulated a set of three culturally orientated questions (pp. 2–3):

1) To what extent can it be demonstrated historically at what time certain peoples either inhabited the areas where such antiquities are found or entered them on war or trading expeditions?
2) What historical traditions do we have that this or that people preferably made or used certain metals and metal compositions of a certain form and chemical composition and for what purposes?
3) If it can be proven that different peoples made metal compositions of similar or the same chemical composition, which people made them earlier? at what time? and what is the chemical constitution of these ancient metal masses?

Critically, he noticed that Greek metal contained tin but no zinc, but Roman contained either tin or zinc. He used this criterion to identify the source and period of the metal finds in Northern European graves. Although we can now see that this is an oversimplification, it marks a major step in our social interpretation of the composition of ancient metals.

His first question is effectively the first published articulation of the concept of archaeological provenance, albeit articulated within the hyper-diffusionist model of cultural transfer prevalent at the time (see Section 4). This idea crystallized further in the mid 19th century into the theory of what was to become provenance studies. The clearest statement of this comes not from metal studies but from stone, in a pair of papers published by Augustin-Alexis Damour (1808–1902). Damour (1865: 313) stated that:

> Lorsqu'on découvre . . ., un objet sur lequel la main de l'homme a marqu son travail, et dont la matière est de provenance lointaine ou étrangère à la contrée, on en infère qu'il y a eu transport de l'objet même, ou du moins de la matière don't il est formé.
>
> When we discover . . ., an object on which the hand of man has marked its work, and whose material is of distant origin or foreign to the region, we infer that there was transport of the object itself, or at least of the matter from which it is formed.

This is essentially the definition of the provenance hypothesis – if an object can be confirmed to be of distant origin, then the only conclusion is that either the object or the raw material must have been transported to the region. Until the early 20th century, however, chemical analyses were generally carried out by gravimetry (wet chemistry) as already described, which required large amounts of sample and considerable skill to produce adequate analyses. Consequently, studies involving a large number of samples were limited – the largest compilation until the early 20th century of copper alloy analyses was that of von Bibra (1869), which reported 1,249 metal analyses from 91 different analysts, of which 602 were his own. By this time gravimetric analysis was capable of measuring at least 11 elements in copper alloys (Cu, Sn, Zn, Pb, Ag, Fe, Sb, As, Ni, Co, S), at levels down to between 0.01% and 0.1%, depending on the element, although subsequent work has suggested that some of von Bibra's trace element data (especially Ni) are unreliable (Caley, 1939: 82).

With the advent of instrumental means of chemical analysis from the early 20th century onwards, and even more intensely following the Second World War, large numbers of archaeological objects could be systematically analysed, and several large-scale projects began, initially on copper alloys, but subsequently on ceramics and lithic materials. The earliest form of instrumental analysis was termed optical emission analysis, which was based on experiments involving the emission of light resulting from heating or sparking gases and solids carried out by Kirchoff and Bunsen (1860). The first spectrometers were used in the iron industry for the detection of trace elements by 1880, but the earliest paper on the analysis of archaeological metal was not published until 1921 (Baudoin, 1921). The replacement of gravimetry by spectroscopy was by no means instantaneous. Earle Radcliffe Caley (1900–1988), one of the leading archaeometallurgists of the 20th century, and also an outstanding historian of metallurgy (translating many of the Medieval and later texts already discussed), clearly preferred gravimetry to the instrumental methods available at the time, even into the 1960s. In his compilation of the analyses of ancient metals (Caley, 1964), he devotes 13 pages to a detailed description of gravimetric methods for the analysis of copper alloys and corrosion products (pp. 81–93), compared to 5 on emission spectrography (pp. 93–97). The reasons are not hard to understand, even though instrumental methods of chemical analysis provided a step-change in the scale of the application of analytical chemistry, in terms of the speed of analysis, sample throughput, and also in the range of trace elements measurable. A key advantage of gravimetry is that each precipitation, when carried out correctly, gives an independent estimate of the quantity of a particular element in the sample. If all elements present in the sample (above, say, 0.01%) are measured, then the sum (the analytical total) of all the estimates should be very close to 100%. The quality of the analysis can therefore be verified by the proximity of the total to 100%. Caley, in his analysis of some Chinese bronzes, labelled the averaged totals of duplicate analyses combining gravimetric and spectrographic analyses for such alloys as ‘satisfactory’ if the total was greater than 99.85%, ‘less satisfactory’ for totals around 99.65%, and ‘much less so’ at 99.3% (Caley *et al.*, 1979: 187). In principle, instrumental methods are capable of similar levels of accuracy, and some modern analyses do approach these values, but often it is not possible to recover a truly independent analytical total because of internal corrections and iterations within the calibration software. The combined protocol of gravimetry for major elements and spectrometry for trace elements employed by Caley in his later work was in fact very common in the major programmes of chemical analysis for archaeological materials carried out in Germany, the Soviet Union, and China up until the 1980s or even later. This involved measuring the major elements gravimetrically (in copper alloys, this included Cu, Sn, Pb, Zn, and often Fe), but quantifying the trace elements (usually including As, Sb, Ni, Ag, and sometimes Bi, Co, and Au) by optical emission spectrometry. It is, of course, the case that trace elements below 0.01% in the sample cannot be measured by gravimetric methods without taking very large samples, and are more easily quantifiable by modern sensitive instrumental methods of analysis.

4 The Archaeological Framework

The period from around the 1950s saw a blossoming of many scientific techniques in archaeology ranging from botany and geophysics to zoology, partly stimulated by the advent and impact of radiocarbon dating from the middle of the century. This gave rise to a ‘Golden Age’ of archaeological materials analysis, in which the developing field of materials science was applied across a range of archaeological materials in order to answer a number of basic questions around the physical nature of objects, and particularly to understand the technological processes involved in their production. A large part of this 'Golden Age' was also devoted to the provenance of materials, particularly after the development of mass spectrometry for isotopes of lead in the 1970s (sometimes termed 'isotope archaeology', to parallel isotope geology). Although the intellectual roots of provenance can be traced back to the mid 19th century, and a number of large-scale provenance studies using optical emission started in the 1930s, it is probably true to say that these initiatives would not have been as influential had there not been a change in theoretical approaches to archaeological interpretation over the same period.

There are multiple origins across the world for what is now archaeology. When Leonard Woolley (1880–1960) excavated a large number of Mesopotamian artefacts laid out side-by-side, accompanied by cylindrical stone scrolls describing each object in three languages, in his excavations at Ur (modern Iraq) in 1925, he had discovered what has become known as the 'World's First Museum' (Hopkins, 2021: 43). These objects, covering 1,500 years of Mesopotamian history, had been accumulated and displayed by the Neo-Babylonian Princess Ennigaldi-Nanna, High Priestess of Ur, 547–c. 530 BCE. Across the ancient world, objects from earlier occupants of the dynastic throne were highly valued in order to lend credibility to the later occupants. Perhaps the best-documented example of this is to be found in China, where there is a long tradition of connoisseurship focussed on the objects of the past, especially those with inscriptions. The most obvious manifestation of attempts to inherit credibility is the rise of the Song Antiquarian Movement during the second half of the 11th century CE of the Song dynasty (960–1279 CE), stimulated both by scholarly curiosity but also by the desire of the Imperial Court to recreate the rituals of former dynasties, and hence reinforce perceptions of cultural continuity and heavenly authority (Sena, 2019). The famous Song scholar-official Ouyang Xiu (欧阳修; 1007–1072 CE) collected inscriptions from bronzes, stone stelae, and rock carvings, including purchasing bronzes from excavations or antique shops. His collection, numbering a thousand ink rubbings of inscriptions, covered the time period from the 10th century BCE King Mu of the Western Zhou dynasty through to the Five Dynasties immediately preceding the Song, and was published in his *Records of Collecting Antiquity* (歐陽文忠公文集) in 1062 CE. The Song dynasty also saw the publication of the oldest surviving illustrated catalogues of antiquities, including the *Illustrated Investigations of Antiquity* (考古圖; 1092 CE) by Lü Dalin (呂大臨; c. 1042-c. 1090).

In Europe, Classical Archaeology (the archaeology of the literate Mediterranean world) can be traced back to the revival of interest in the art of the classical world in late Renaissance Italy (15th century CE) and the subsequent rise of the 'Grand

Tour' amongst the elites of western Europe. By the 18th century, no noble house was complete without a cabinet of curiosities, consisting of specimens of geological, archaeological, and mythological origin, in part collected during tours of southern Europe, and, following Napoleon's campaign of 1798–1801, Egypt. A separate branch of European archaeology, leading to prehistoric archaeology, began as an antiquarian pastime for the wealthy, with many burial mounds and other structures, often on their own estates, being opened to recover the 'treasures' therein. As in China, a more structured approach to the buried past was given in England by the need of the Tudor State to emphasize its connections with the mythological past, signified by the appointment of John Leland (1503–1552) as King's Antiquary in 1533 (Trigger, 1989). This paved the way for the publication in 1586 of *Britannia* by William Camden (1551–1623), providing a survey of what was then known about Roman England, John Aubrey's (1626–1697) *Monumenta Britannica*, written between 1665 and 1693 and originally existing as two manuscripts (Bodleian MS Top. Gen. c. 24–5) but not published until 1980 (Legg and Fowles, 1980), and the well-known work of William Stukeley (1687–1765) at Stonehenge and elsewhere, including *Stonehenge. A Temple Restor'd to the British Druids*, published in 1740.

This period of archaeology is generally known as the antiquarian stage. With increasing professionalization (or, before that, the emergence of a number of privately sponsored scholars, such as Giovanni Belzoni (1778–1823), Sir Austin Henry Layard (1817–1894), Heinrich Schliemann (1822–1890), Sir Marc Aurel Stein (1862–1943), and Howard Carter (1874–1939)), a newer philosophical framework emerged, termed culture-historical archaeology. This used material assemblages to define distinct cultures, often with ethnic and nationalistic overtones. Drawing heavily on emerging theories of Darwinian evolution and its anthropological interpretations, this began to see the many prehistoric and modern 'primitive societies' as stages on the inevitable progression from 'barbarism' to 'civilization'. Crucially, the dominant view was that such societies were incapable of advancing themselves from internal forces, and that the primary mechanism of technological change was the diffusion of ideas from outside. This culminated in the so-called hyperdiffusionist philosophies, which postulated that the major advances in human society (e.g., farming, tool use, metallurgy, but also cultural practices such as embalming) emerged once only (often attributed to ancient Egypt), and diffused throughout the world. The most obvious proponent of such ideas was the Australian anatomist and Egyptologist Grafton Elliot Smith (1871–1937), who published a number of influential volumes, including *The Ancient Egyptians and the Origin of Civilization* (1911), *The Migrations of Early Culture* (1915), and *The Diffusion of Culture* (1933). He argued, for example, that the practices of artificial mummification began in Egypt and spread across the world, ultimately influencing the Inca in south America (Elliot-Smith, 1916).

This idea of cultural stasis, only changed by the arrival of people and ideas from elsewhere, was heavily rooted in the self-perception of the colonial powers during the 18th and 19th centuries, who believed that colonization was a mechanism for the improvement of the colonized. These views have since been refuted by the multiple freedom movements of the 20th century, reinvigorating the study of many indigenous cultures, from the Amazon to the subcontinent of India. Associated with this was the rise of processual (or 'New') archaeology in the 1960s, which recognized that isolated cultures were capable of internal evolutionary processes (Trigger, 1989). Much greater emphasis was placed on understanding the ecological, technological, economic, and social forces experienced by ancient societies. This was in part enabled by the increasing adoption within archaeology of scientific methodologies developed elsewhere, including palaeoenvironmental techniques (pollen, plant macrofossils, and zooarchaeological analysis) and dating techniques, starting with the 'radiocarbon revolution' from the 1950s onwards. Material analysis also became part of this New Archaeology, enabling the detailed study of technological processes from a physical and chemical examination of the artefacts themselves, but also from the characterization of production debris, residual manufacturing structures, and also the raw materials (see, for example, several chapters in Pollard *et al.*, 2023a).

Thus, the mid 19th century idea of provenance found a fertile environment within the New Archaeology. Although originating within a strong cultural diffusionist framework, where the identification of intrusive material objects was taken as indications of the presence of external influences, the theory rapidly morphed into a new model, although with little overt self-reflection (exceptions include Weigand *et al.* (1977) in the context of turquoise, Hunt (2012) for ceramics and Pernicka (2014) for metals). The emphasis on economic factors as being part of the evolutionary pressure on society meant that the identification of trade (interpreted in its widest sense) became an important part of archaeological research. Fortuitously, this combined with the increased availability of instrumental analytical methods to allow the initiation of several massive programmes on the chemical analysis of archaeological artefacts.

5 Provenance in Practice

There is no standard methodology for carrying out a successful provenance study, but there are some broad general principles. The first requirement is the generation of a meaningful starting hypothesis. For example, the question 'where do these objects come from' is strictly speaking unanswerable, since it implies a comprehensive knowledge of all the possible sources available at the time of manufacture, which is unlikely for a number of reasons, including the sparseness of such data, and the possibility that viable ancient sources remain unknown. In contrast, 'do these objects (X) come from A, B or C' is a more straightforward question, provided sufficient and representative (control) samples are available from sources A, B, or C. The answer, however, should take the form 'given the data available for sources A, B or C, source A (or whichever) is the most likely source for X, providing that there is no similar but unknown source'. It might be possible using multivariate statistics or kernel density modelling to assign a probability to the proposal that X comes from A, B, or C, but it should be recognized that these probabilities are conditional on the variables measured and the samples analysed. Similar constraints apply to provenance-to-match questions – 'do these two groups of objects have the same characteristics' is in principle answerable, but it is important to recognize that, statistically speaking, differences can be established to a required degree of probability, whereas similarity has to be inferred. This means that if a match between X and A is determined to have a low probability (i.e., below a specified critical value), then it can safely be assumed that X and A are different. If, however, the similarity between X and A is accepted at a certain degree of probability (usually 95% confidence), it cannot be assumed that X and A are the same – only that, according to the variables measured and the number of samples analysed, X is *consistent* with A. It is then up to the person interpreting the data to decide whether, taking all possible sources of evidence into consideration, it is reasonable to accept the hypothesis that they are the same. Such additional evidence might include technological (e.g., are they made in the same way?), archaeological (e.g., is the distribution of objects of type X the same as that of type A?), or art historical (e.g., do A and X use identical decorative motifs and techniques?).

Once the hypothesis to be tested has been established, it is then necessary to decide on the mode of analysis, and the interpretational technique(s) to be used. Clearly, the choice of analytical technique dictates the range of elements or isotopes that can be determined, and hence defines the fingerprint available. The earlier analytical techniques (gravimetry, optical emission (OES), atomic absorption (AAS)) have been completely replaced by a range of newer methods, including inductively coupled plasma methods (ICP-AES or ICP-MS), which in general offer a wider range of measurable elements, with higher sensitivities (i.e., lower minimum detectable levels) allowing much lower levels of certain elements to be measured, combined with faster sample throughput and lower levels of sampling damage. Neutron activation analysis (NAA), which was the benchmark technique for many years for the measurement of trace elements, has now virtually disappeared because of the lack of access to nuclear reactors, but has also largely been replaced by ICP techniques. Other methods available include X-ray fluorescence (XRF) and electron microscopy (SEM, electron microprobe, and so on). Each method has its own strengths and weaknesses, which must be evaluated in the context of the research question being addressed, not least of which is to ask whether a particular technique is capable of measuring the elements (or isotopes) most likely to provide a fingerprint with sufficient sensitivity and precision. For a more detailed description of these techniques as they are used in archaeology, see Pollard *et al.* (2007).

Likewise, there is no simple rule to define the 'best' approach for any particular material. It is generally accepted that, for manufactured materials (e.g., metal, glass, and ceramic), it is better to focus on minor (0.1–1%), trace (0.001–0.1%), or ultra-trace elements (<0.001%), since the major elements (>1%)[1] tend to be deliberately controlled for physical or aesthetic reasons. Within the trace and ultra-trace elements, the rare earth elements (REE) provide a special set of elements consisting of the lanthanides (La, Ce, Pr, Nd, Pm, Sm, Eu, Gd, Tb, Dy, Ho, Er, Tm, Yb, and Lu), often supplemented by Y and Sc, which have virtually indistinguishable chemical properties, but provide a graded series of atomic numbers (from 57 to 71) and hence gradually increasing ionic radius (size). Because of this chemical similarity but size differential, the series is often systematically fractionated by particular geochemical processes – sometimes to enhance the lighter elements (LREE), and sometimes the heavier (HREE) – and thus are often used in geochemistry to elucidate processes (Henderson, 1984). They therefore also provide a promising starting point for archaeological provenance studies, especially for ceramics and glass. They are, however, rarely used as measured, since there is a strong odd-even (atomic number) effect, meaning that a plot of the REE's in, say, a clay would show a sawtooth profile. To counter this, it is usual to normalize the REE profile using the abundance of the REE's in a specified chondrite (stony meteorite, representing primeval composition). Providing all data have been normalized to the same chondrite, REE profiles can be directly compared. Another powerful method in geochemistry using selected trace elements is the practice of plotting Nb/Ta against Zr/Hf, particularly in granitic rocks, but also in ore deposits (Dostal and Chatterjee, 2000). Zirconium (Zr) and hafnium (Hf) are d-block transition metals with the same outer electron configuration but in successive periods – hence, they have very similar chemical properties but

[1] There is no uniform definition of these terms, but these levels are typical of those used in archaeology.

different atomic weights (40 and 72, respectively), and therefore the ratio of their abundances, just as with the REE series, provide a sensitive process indicator. The same is true of niobium (Nb) and tantalum (Ta). Plotting the two ratios together can be a very effective way of studying the evolution of the continental crust. Little use so far has been made of these particular ratios in archaeology, but similar elemental ratios have been used effectively for the discrimination between sands of different sources, used to manufacture glass (Degryse, 2014: 71). Perhaps the most influential pair of ratios to date has been 1000Zr/Ti plotted against Cr/La (Shortland *et al.*, 2007: fig. 6; Walton *et al.*, 2009), which has been shown to discriminate between early Mesopotamian and Egyptian glass – an important tool in the discussion about the origin of glass. Titanium (Ti) and Zr form a pair similar to Zr and Hf; chromium (Cr) and lanthanum (La) do not form such a pair (both are d-block transition elements, but not from adjacent periods, and having different valence), but Cr is generally associated with iron minerals, and La with clay minerals. As such, this pair of elemental ratios has also proved useful in archaeological studies of glass.

Most, but not all, elements exist in more than one isotopic form. An isotope is an atom which has the same atomic number (number of protons in the nucleus) but a different number of neutrons, giving different atomic weights. Since atomic number dictates the chemistry of the element, isotopes have identical chemical properties, but different weights, which gives rise to variation in those properties which depend on kinetics. For example, carbon (C) is defined as that element which has six protons in the nucleus, but it has three isotopes: carbon-12 (^{12}C), with six protons and six neutrons; carbon-13 (^{13}C), with six protons and seven neutrons; and the radioactive carbon-14 (^{14}C), with six protons and eight neutrons. The most common of these isotopes is ^{12}C, which constitutes 99% of all C, followed by ^{13}C, which is around 1%, and the radioactively unstable isotope is very rare, consisting of about one atom in a million million (1 in 10^{12}) of ^{12}C.

Following the first experimental confirmation of the existence of isotopes (in the gas neon) by Francis William Aston (1877–1945) in Cambridge, UK (Aston, 1920a), between 1920 and 1925 Aston produced a spectacular series of seven papers on the mass spectrometry of an increasing number of elements. In 1920, the number of elements whose precise atomic weight (and hence number of stable isotopes) was known was 11 (Aston, 1920b). By 1925, 56 elements were listed (over half of the 80 non-radioactive elements known), including many metals (Fe, Co, Ni, Cu, Zn, Ag, Sn, Sb, Ba, Hg), but not lead (Aston, 1925). The four stable isotopes of lead (^{204}Pb, ^{206}Pb, ^{207}Pb, and ^{208}Pb) were first measured by Nier in 1938. This was particularly important for isotope geochemistry, since three of these lead isotopes (^{206}Pb, ^{207}Pb, and ^{208}Pb) are end members of the uranium (^{238}U and ^{235}U) and thorium (^{232}Th) radioactive decay chains. Hence the natural variation in lead isotopes is much greater than for other isotopes, and also measuring isotope ratios within these decay chains provides some of the fundamental isotope geochronometers in the earth sciences (e.g., Faure, 1986).

The idea of using variation in lead isotope ratios for provenancing archaeological objects was presented by Robert H. Brill (1929–2021) and Jesse Marion Wampler at a meeting held in Boston, USA, entitled *Application of Science in the Examination of Works of Art*, in September 1965, published in 1967 (Brill and Wampler, 1967a). Before this appeared in print, Grögler *et al.* (1966) published the lead isotopic analysis of ten Roman lead pipes and ingots from across Europe, comparing these data with ores from the UK, Germany, Austria, Italy, Jugoslavia, Portugal, Spain, and Greece, thus staking the claim to be the first published lead isotope study in archaeology. Two archaeological samples from Portugal, for example, found matches – one with ores from the southern Algarve and the other with Rio Tinto. These and similar matches were sufficient for the authors to observe that archaeological lead objects could be matched with potential ore sources. The larger and better-known publication of lead isotopes on archaeological materials is that of Brill and Wampler (1967b), who reported carrying out 230 measurements, of which 70 were on lead ores (from Greece (Laurion), England, and Spain) and 160 on lead from archaeological samples, with the explicit purpose of establishing the provenance of the artefacts. The catalogue of the samples reported in this particular paper only lists 36 archaeological metals, all of which are lead objects, apart from one (no. 188), which was lead extracted from a Chinese early Zhou dynasty bronze vessel, the results of which were found to be 'entirely different from the leads found in any of the other archaeological samples studied' (Brill and Wampler, 1967b: 76). The actual measurements are not given in the paper. A further eight results are discussed, consisting of seven from samples of glass, and one from the glaze of a Roman vessel from Caerleon, Wales (UK).

Although these papers established beyond doubt the potential for lead isotope analysis on archaeological artefacts, the principal focus was on lead objects, which are relatively rare from archaeological contexts. Sample 188 (the Zhou dynasty bronze) in Brill and Wampler (1967b) showed that sufficient lead could be extracted from bronze for isotope measurement, but that sample contained 11.6% lead, which is much higher than in most European Bronze Age bronzes. It was not until the late 1970s that extraction of traces of lead from copper (and silver) alloys was routinely established, allowing the method to become a major contributor to provenance studies of non-ferrous metals, especially in the Mediterranean (Gale and Stos-Gale, 1982). Isotopic data (most commonly lead, but more recently a wider range of elements such as tin, copper, antimony, strontium, boron, and so on) now provide an extra dimension (in that the isotopic values are generally independent of the abundance of the element), which can be used either in combination with trace elements or alone.

With the increased capacity for generating chemical (and subsequently isotopic) data from archaeological samples, interpretation of the subsequent data became an increasingly pressing problem. In the early days of instrumental chemical analysis, ingenious ways were developed to compare large sets of data. In ceramics, for example, the datasets provided by OES or AAS typically contained abundances of 10 or 12 elements (expressed conventionally as oxides), typically including SiO_2, TiO_2, Al_2O_3, CaO, MgO, Na_2O, K_2O, FeO, and MnO_2, plus a few trace elements (e.g., Cr, Ni, and so on). One obvious approach is to display the data as a set of bi-plots – CaO versus MgO, Na_2O versus K_2O, and so on. This can be extremely effective if the analyst hits upon the 'right' set of plots; but with nine elements measured, there are 36 possible combinations of bi-plot, which would have been laborious to plot at the time. In an attempt to consider all elements at the same time, a system was devised in which they were presented as a set of logarithm-scale columns, one for each element (oxide), sometimes multiplied by an arbitrary number to bring the data into range. Thus, Figure 2 (from Catling and Jones, 1977) shows a comparison of ceramic data from Chania (Crete) with the so-called Theban Stirrup Jars (TSJ). The shaded area for each column represents the 80% confidence level for each element, with the horizontal bar representing the mean (average) concentration.

Such plots (and variations on the same theme) seem cumbersome now, but did have a number of advantages in a pre-computer era. A visual match can be made by comparing equivalent columns for each dataset, and a match would be accepted if the majority of columns appeared to cover the same range – this was elegantly expressed in this case as 'TSJ compositions can be collectively accommodated within the Chania characteristics.' Alternative presentations, in which the set of elements are horizontally linked by a band joining the averages and upper and lower limits, which could then be superimposed from different assemblages, allowed such comparisons to be made more easily. The method could also be extended to other sets of data, such as the composition of copper alloys, or glasses (e.g., Figure 3). There is naturally a degree of subjectivity in deciding when the columns or ribbons 'match', but it does allow for the range of variation in each set of data, rather than simply relying on comparing averages. On the other hand, because of correlations between elements, it probably overemphasizes the matching (or non-matching) between the sets of data, since it treats each element as fully independent.

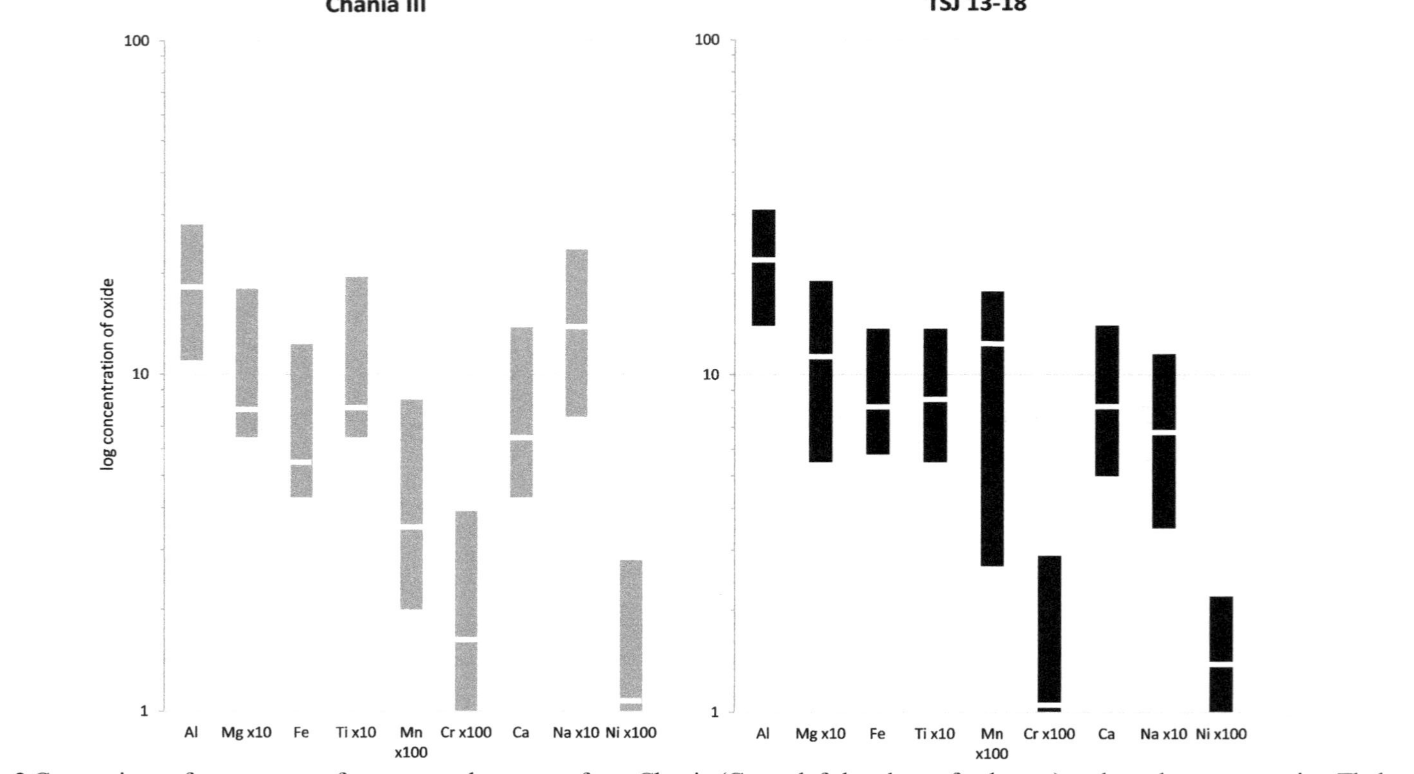

Figure 2 Comparison of two groups of pottery analyses, one from Chania (Crete: left-hand set of columns) and another representing Theban Stirrup Jars (TSJ's: right-hand set). The coloured area for each oxide represents the concentration range associated with an 80% level of confidence, and the white bar within each area is the mean concentration. Note that the vertical axis is logarithmic, and that some oxides are multiplied by 10 or 100 for ease of presentation. Discrimination is made by visual pairwise comparison – in this case, most pairs overlap, but Mn is higher in TSJ and both Cr and Na are higher in Chania III. Redrawn from fig. 1f in Catling and Jones (1977).

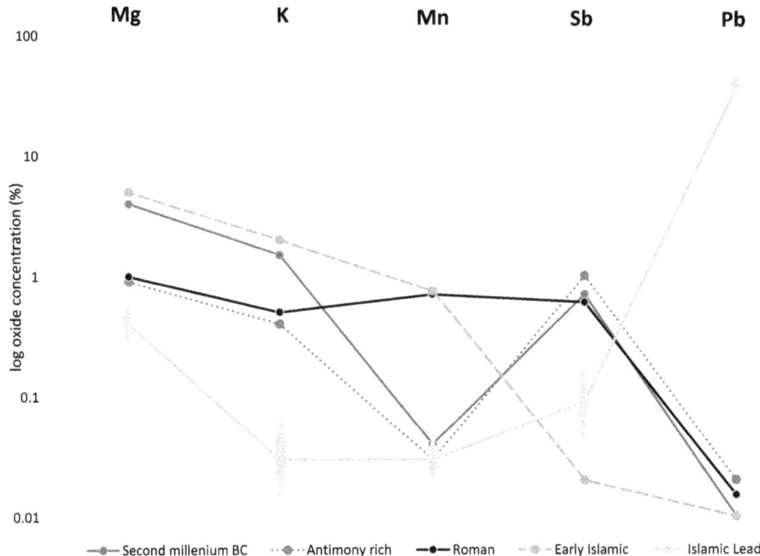

Figure 3 Comparison of five oxides in five important types of Old World glass, redrawn from Sayre and Smith (1961; fig. 1). For each glass type (2nd millennium BC, Antimony rich), the five horizontal lines link the mean composition for each glass type, enabling similarities and differences to be easily seen. For Islamic lead only, the lozenge indicates the mean value for that element, and the vertical extent of the lozenge shows the standard deviation for that element (the standard deviations are omitted from the other types for clarity).

Such visual attempts to match these datasets were gradually replaced during the 1970s by an avowedly multivariate approach based on treating each measured element (or oxide) as a variable in a multivariate space defined by these variables – essentially treating each analysed sample as a point in multivariate space, with coordinates equal to the value of the concentration of each element. This approach was applied particularly following the rise of NAA, which was capable of measuring many more elements simultaneously than OES or AAS, thus requiring a more sophisticated approach to data analysis. It was also, of course, enabled by the availability of computers capable of dealing with the calculations required. Multivariate techniques, such as hierarchical cluster analysis (CA) and principal components analysis (PCA) (Hodson, 1969) and Mahalanobis distance-based metrics (Bieber *et al.,* 1976) began to be applied to archaeometric data (Glascock and MacDonald, 2023). Such methods have been incorrectly described as multivariate statistics, which in general they are not. Mainly they provide methods for dimensional reduction, which allow high-dimensional data to be reduced to fewer dimensions, so that the data can be presented in two dimensions (i.e., can be printed) with minimal distortion of the relational information. In some versions (e.g., discriminant function analysis, DFA, and more recently Bayesian and kernel density methods: Pollard *et al.*, 2023b), probabilities of group membership can be generated, but these are only valid in the context of the data presented. Although more rigorous statistical tests can be applied to evaluate the discrimination between multivariate groups, such as Hotellings-T^2 test – the multivariate extension of Student's t-test – they are rarely, if ever, used in archaeology.

Figure 4, from Hodson (1969), shows a redrawn dendrogram resulting from the clustering of 100 analyses of European bronzes published as part of the SAM project (see below: 90 published by Junghans *et al.* (1960) and 10 by Schubert and Schubert (1967)). The data consisted of 11 elements (Sn, Pb, As, Sb, Ag, Ni, Bi, Au, Zn, Co, and Fe), and the distance between the samples was measured by squared-mean Euclidean distance (SMED). Clustering was by average-link cluster analysis (ALCA). The dendrogram is plotted with the 100 samples numbered from left to right across the top, with increasing dissimilarity (decreasing similarity) plotted downwards. Hodson identified 16 clusters (as numbered across the top), and subsequently plotted the samples belonging to each group on a map of Europe. He concluded that the method had 'performed surprisingly well'. It is important to note, however, that the choice of distance metric and clustering algorithm can drastically affect the appearance of the dendrogram (Pollard, 1983), which is itself a 2D representation of (in this case) 11-dimensional data, and will therefore be distorted to some degree.

Isotopic data, initially the three ratios recorded in lead isotope analysis, present a different set of problems, but came with an already-standardized presentation format, derived from isotope geochronology. This consisted of producing a pair of plots – in the early days of archaeological applications (Brill and Wampler, 1967b), these were $^{206}Pb/^{204}Pb$ versus $^{206}Pb/^{207}Pb$, and $^{208}Pb/^{207}Pb$ versus $^{206}Pb/^{207}Pb$. Because the $^{206}Pb/^{207}Pb$ axis is common to both figures, Brill and Wampler plotted these two one above the other (redrawn in Figure 5, to better separate the two plots). In this particular figure, archaeological objects of lead from Sardinia, England, and Greece are plotted against specific ore samples, and estimated ore fields defined by modern mineral samples from ancient mining regions. The ore fields are marked as ellipses labelled L (Laurion, Greece), S (Spain), and E (England), although it was observed at the time that, because of the low resolution of the measurements and the low number of samples, these attributions are uncertain since group L, for example, also contains ores from Iran. The interpretation of lead isotope data stimulated a great deal of debate during the 1980s and 1990s, and subsequently alternative modes of presentation have been proposed to bring out the

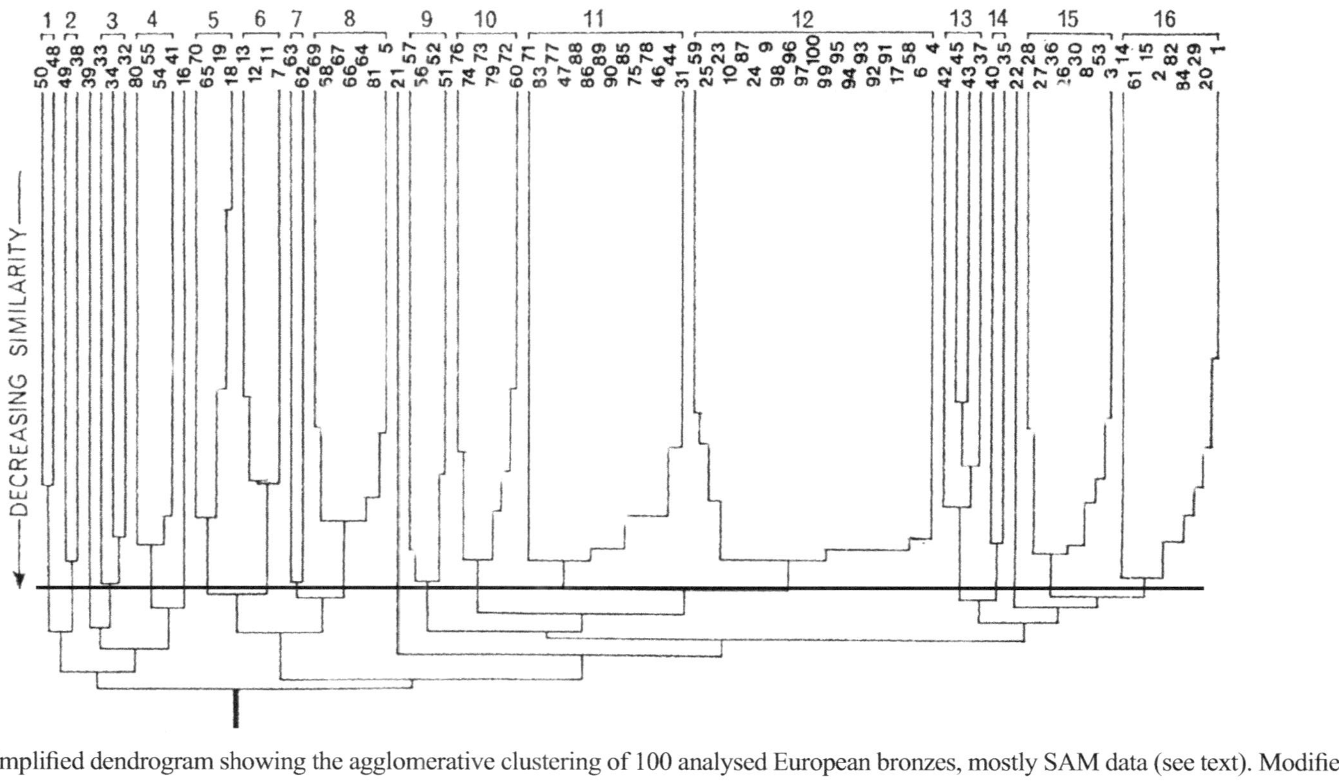

Figure 4 Simplified dendrogram showing the agglomerative clustering of 100 analysed European bronzes, mostly SAM data (see text). Modified from Hodson (1969). Sample numbers are listed horizontally, below the 16 groups identified by Hodson. Similarity between samples decreases down the diagram – horizontal ties mark the dissimilarity between adjacent samples or groups. For clarity, the linkages within the larger groups have been deleted. The dark horizontal line shows the level of dissimilarity identified as significant by Hodson. This is often arbitrary, and a small number of samples are ungrouped at this level (samples 39, 21, and 22).

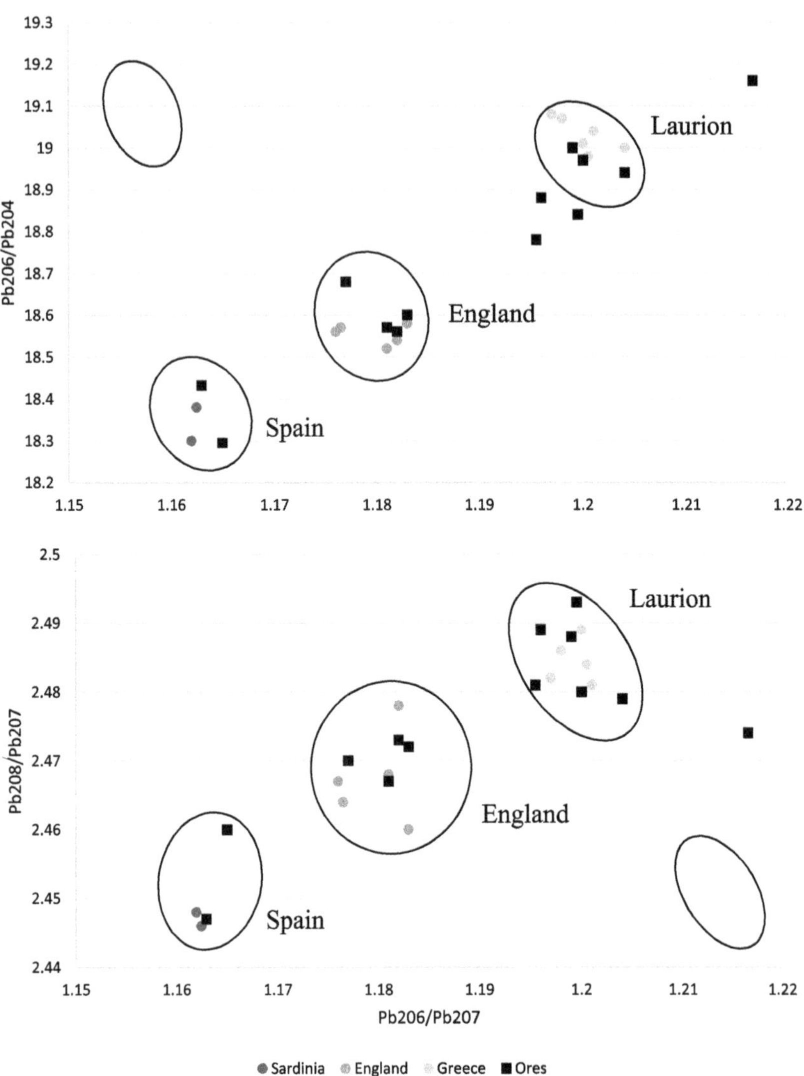

Figure 5 Early plot of lead isotope data on archaeological lead samples, compared to various ores fields. Redrawn from Brill and Wampler (1967b; ill. 2). Lower diagram plots $^{208}Pb/^{207}Pb$ versus $^{206}Pb/^{207}Pb$ for 13 archaeological lead samples (from Sardinia, England, and Greece) plus 13 lead ore samples, from Sardinia, England, and Laurion, Greece. Upper diagram plots $^{206}Pb/^{204}Pb$ versus $^{206}Pb/^{207}Pb$ for same samples. Unlabelled ellipses indicate estimated measurement errors at the time.

archaeological rather that the geological context of the samples, such as plotting the inverse concentration of lead against one of the lead isotopic ratios (1/Pb versus $^{206}Pb/^{204}Pb$) (Pollard and Bray, 2015).

6 The 'Golden Age' of Provenance Studies

This section is intended to briefly outline some of the major provenance projects undertaken over the last 100 years, without pretending to be either comprehensive or conclusive. It takes a deliberately historical approach, rather than attempting to summarize the latest work, since this allows the development of the intellectual underpinnings to be examined. The approach is by material, rather than by archaeological culture, geographical region or time period. This is because, although the archaeological context of the question is all-important, the practical constraints are largely dictated by the nature of the material being studied, and it is therefore preferable to think about the theory of provenance studies from the perspective of each material.

It has long been realized that different materials pose different challenges in terms of the complexity of any proposed provenance study. In principle, natural lithic materials present the least problems in this context – most lithic materials require little or no extractive processing other than digging or cutting out, individual objects cannot be made from mixed (different) sources without the fact being obvious, and lithics offer limited opportunities for recycling into new objects, apart from the process of reduction, by which a tool is reshaped or resharpened. None of these processes are likely to alter the chemical or isotopic composition of the object, thereby reducing considerably the potential constraints on provenance. This is clearly not the case with manufactured materials – principally ceramics, metals, faience, and glass. The simple fact that the raw materials have to be extracted, processed, and manufactured at high temperatures suggests that there may be some issues with the relative stability of the 'fingerprints' from source to artefact. Beyond this, there is the obvious potential for raw materials from different sources to be mixed, and for some finished materials (particularly metals and glass) to be recycled. A fuller discussion of the impact of these factors on the theory of provenance is deferred to the succeeding sections.

6.1 Lithics

Interest in the provenance of the stones of megalithic monuments has a very long history, and probably represents one of the earliest scientific analyses in archaeology. Stukeley (1740: 5) reports the microscopic examination of fragments of stone from Stonehenge carried out by himself at the Royal Society, London, on samples collected by Halley in 1720. He concludes that the stones came from 'the gray weathers, upon Marlborough downs', but the altar and 'pyramidals' are much harder, and from elsewhere. Thus began 250 years of research into the geological origin of the 'bluestones' at Stonehenge – now agreed to be the Preseli Hills in west Wales, some 180 miles (290 km) from Stonehenge (Parker Pearson *et al.*, 2019). This, of course, then gave rise to the question of how such large stones were transported over these distances in the Neolithic.

Obviously, worked stone tools have been a major indicator of human activity since the beginning of the human species. Since not all types of stone are equally suitable for chipping and shaping, it is inevitable that particular sources began to be favoured for tool production. Thus, identifying the geological source of the stone gives invaluable information about human behaviour, although in such cases it is quite likely that visual or petrological identification might be sufficient to achieve this aim.

6.1.1 Flint

This is less true in more homogeneous fine-grained rock such as flint. The first study of prehistoric flint mines in England and northern France was carried out by Sieveking *et al.* (1970) using AAS to measure Al, Mg, K, and Fe in flints from six mine sites, followed by principal components analysis, suggesting that discrimination was possible. The same samples were subsequently re-analysed (along with other samples) by Aspinall and Feather (1972) using NAA to measure 15 trace elements (Na, Cs, Sc, Ta, Cr, Fe, Co, La, Ce, Sm, Eu, Tb, Yb, Th, and U). There was considerable scatter in the data, but it was confirmed that Continental and British sources could be clearly distinguished, based on elements such as Cr and Th. Much of the early work on archaeological flint was summarized at a conference in 1983, published by Sieveking and Hart (1986).

6.1.2 Obsidian

Although strictly a natural volcanic glass rather than a rock, obsidian has been an important medium for the manufacture of bladed tools, traded over considerable distances, and has consequently received considerable attention in terms of provenance. Obsidian tools were also of interest because of the phenomenon known as hydration, in which the alkali elements in the surface are exchanged for hydrogen ions from the water in the surrounding burial environment. The resulting hydration layer (an alkali-depleted hydrated silica gel) can be seen under the optical microscope in cross section, and it has been argued that the thickness of the layer is indicative of the time elapsed since initial exposure. Although it is not necessarily a linear relationship (since ion exchange is a chemical process, and is hence controlled by environmental parameters), obsidian hydration dating is still used in some parts of the world, particularly where organic preservation is poor (Liritzis and Laskaris, 2009).

In terms of provenance, the initial assumption was that each obsidian flow (corresponding to the later stages of a rhyolitic volcanic eruption) should exhibit a unique and homogeneous pattern of trace elements because of the evolution of magma composition during eruption, and hence obsidian flaked from a particular flow should have a unique chemical fingerprint (e.g., Wright, 1968). This combination of geological specificity and long-distance trading makes obsidian a highly attractive target for chemical and isotopic study. Because obsidian is a natural glass, its major element composition (SiO_2, CaO, K_2O, Na_2O, and so on) is constrained by the chemistry of the magma and the physical requirements of the glass transition conditions (largely viscosity), so any variation between flows is expected to be most easily seen in the trace elements. Although early work in the Mediterranean utilized OES methods to measure 16 trace elements, the most significant of which were deemed to be Ba and Zr (Renfrew *et al.*, 1965: see Figure 6), the analytical focus elsewhere rapidly fell on NAA (e.g., Frison *et al.* (1968) in the northwestern plains of the USA, and Gordus *et al.* (1968) from a wide range of geological sources across North America), measuring a range of elements, including Mn, Sc, La, Rb, Sm, Ba, Zr, Na, and Fe. The archaeological significance of these studies is considerable. Gordus *et al.* (1968) point out that obsidian was common on Hopewell sites in the Illinois valley (c. 200 BCE–300 CE), but the nearest sources are in Mexico, New Mexico, Yellowstone National Park, and on the Pacific Coast, the closest of which is 1,500 miles (2,400 km) away. Location to source therefore illustrates the existence of some form of long distance trade networks. Perhaps even more strikingly, in the Mediterranean obsidian was exploited from the early Neolithic onwards (c. 8000 BCE). Moreover, many of the major sources are found on islands (e.g., Sardinia, Lipari, Palmarola, Pantelleria, and Melos), indicating not only long-distance trade in the Neolithic, but also some competence in boat-building and sailing (Dixon *et al.*, 1968).

Like many areas of archaeological science, as more work is done and more data published, the original assumptions can be seen as oversimplifications. This is less the case in obsidian studies than in some other areas, but there is still some ambiguity between potential sources. Gale (1981), for example, pointed out that trace element analysis was not capable of completely resolving the known obsidian sources around the Mediterranean (the islands, plus Anatolian, Armenian, Hungarian, and Slovakian sources), and proposed using the strontium isotope ratio ($^{87}Sr/^{86}Sr$) to discriminate between them, which was one of the first uses of this particular isotope system within archaeology.

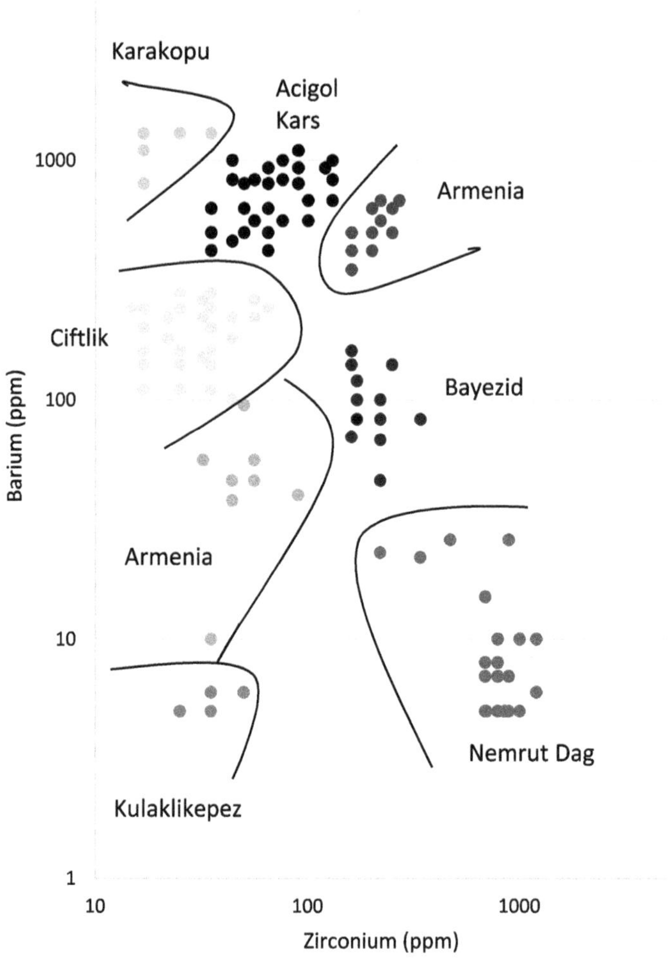

Figure 6 Plot of log concentration of barium versus zirconium as measured by OES from various obsidian sources in the Near East, showing good separation of the major sources. Plotted from data presented in Table 2 of Renfrew *et al.* 1966. Groupings are those proposed by Renfrew *et al.*

This ratio varies geologically because ^{86}Sr is stable, but ^{87}Sr is a daughter of ^{87}Rb, so the $^{87}Sr/^{86}Sr$ ratio varies in geological materials depending on the initial $^{87}Rb/^{86}Sr$ ratio, and the geological age of the deposit. Given that obsidian flows tend to be short-term events, but occurring over a wide range of geological periods, it is likely that different flows, even in the same location, will have different strontium isotope ratios because of magmatic evolution. For the Mediterranean sources of obsidian, a plot of $^{87}Sr/^{86}Sr$ versus Rb gave very good separation, and allowed archaeological samples to be assigned to specific sources. Gale also noted, however, that a plot of Sr versus Rb gave 'completely sufficient' resolution of these sources, and compared this with the rather complicated 'simple discrimination diagrams' produced by Renfrew *et al.* (1965), in which [Li+(Ca/100)+(Mg/10)] was plotted against [(Zr/2)+Nb+Pb+(Fe/100)]. Although these linear combinations seem somewhat arbitrary now, it must be remembered that, prior to principal components analysis and discriminant function analysis, it was quite common to empirically produce such combinations in an attempt to maximize the visual discrimination between source groups.

Despite these complexities, particularly around the Mediterranean, the method of trace element analysis has become so widely accepted that suitably calibrated portable XRF spectrometers can now be used in the field to provenance huge numbers of obsidian artefacts in a very short time (Tykot, 2021).

6.1.3 Marble

Another important lithic material for provenance studies has been marble, used throughout the classical world and elsewhere for public and private architecture, and for statuary. Marble is a metamorphic form of limestone, and has restricted occurrences. Some famous ancient marble quarries, such as Carrara in Tuscany (Italy) or Paros in the Aegean, have continued in use into modern times. The history of provenance studies of classical marble has followed a familiar trajectory, which could be generalized to the history of such studies for most materials, at least in Europe:

- Inferences on provenance made from classical and biblical written sources up to the late 18th century
- Visual examination, leading to microscopy and petrography, starting in the 19th century
- Chemical analysis, starting with gravimetry in the 19th century but leading to spectrography in the mid 20th century
- Trace element analysis by NAA from the mid 20th century, replaced by ICP-MS at the end of the 20th century
- Application of isotope measurements in the later 20th century.

The application of isotope methods came relatively early for archaeological marble. Because marbles are carbonates, and because there had been considerable geological interest in the light stable isotope ratios of carbon ($^{13}C/^{12}C$) and oxygen ($^{18}O/^{16}O$) in marine carbonates, significant success was achieved from a relatively early date using these isotopes in archaeological material (Craig and Craig, 1972). In this study, modern samples of marbles from the ancient quarries of Naxos, Paros, Mount Hymettus, and Mount Pentelikon were separable using these measurements, and archaeological samples from a number of extant monuments were attributed to certain of these sources (see Figure 7).

For the light stable isotopes (e.g., H, C, O, N, S), the data are conventionally reported as δ values, in which the specified ratio in a sample is converted to a value relative to the same ratio in an agreed international standard material, in units of parts per thousand (referred to as 'per mil', ‰). For carbon, the ratio is $^{13}C/^{12}C$, and for oxygen it is $^{18}O/^{16}O$, and the standard material for these isotopes in inorganic carbonates is PDB (Pee-Dee Belemnite), a fossil bivalve from the Cretaceous Peedee formation in South Carolina, USA. The definition is:

$$\delta(‰) = \left[\frac{R - R^*}{R^*}\right] \times 1,000,$$

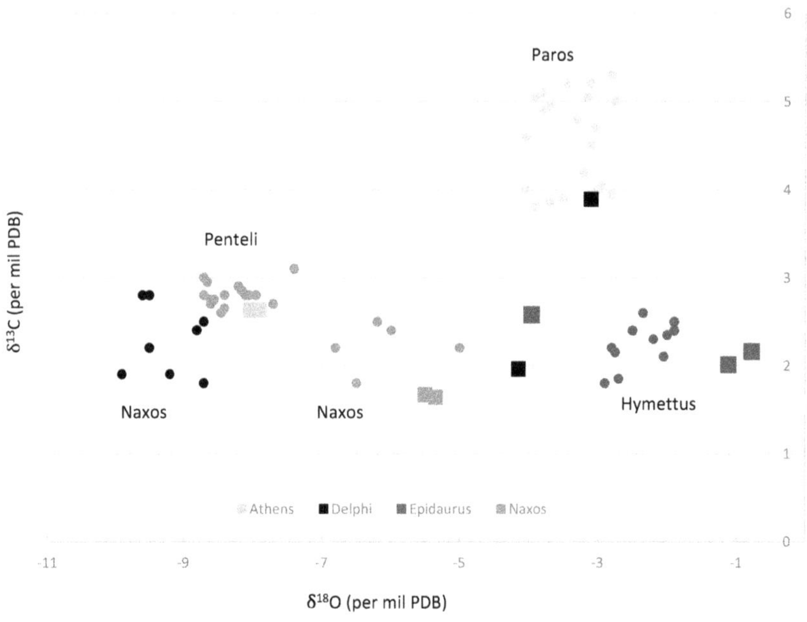

Figure 7 Stable isotope analyses ($\delta^{13}C$ versus $\delta^{18}O$) of modern samples from four ancient sources of marble (circles: Naxos, Penteli, Paros, and Hymettus), with eight archaeological marble samples (squares). The two archaeological samples from Athens are associated with the group for Penteli; one of the two from Delphi is assigned to Paros, and both samples from Naxos are close to one of the two groups identified as Naxos. The other three are unattributed. Based on data presented in fig. 1 and table 1 of Craig and Craig (1972).

where R is the ratio in the sample and R^* the ratio in the standard. Figure 7 is a plot of $\delta^{13}C$ versus $\delta^{18}O$ for five of the major marble sources around the Mediterranean, showing very good discrimination.

6.2 Ceramics

The scientific study of ceramics began in Europe in the early 18th century with the analysis of samples of a miraculous material obtained from China – porcelain – including both the raw materials and the finished products (Pollard, 2015). This was important for many reasons, not least of which was the stimulus that it provided for the analysis of archaeological ceramics. One of the early English contributors to such a study was Simeon Shaw (1785–1859), who produced a volume entitled *The Chemistry of the Several Natural and Artificial Heterogeneous Compounds Used in Manufacturing Porcelain, Glass, and Pottery* (Shaw, 1837). The publication of this volume was supported by 250 subscribers, including many of the leading ceramic producers in Staffordshire, and, in the introduction, Shaw states that it 'results from the wish for Science to perfect the Manufactures of Porcelain, Pottery, and Glass'. This dedication might well be true, but it was equally motivated by the wish to enable English manufacturers to compete with the great factories on the Continent, especially Sèvres, of which Shaw was certainly aware: his work references the forthcoming publication of Alexandre Brongniart's monumental work (*Traité des Arts Céramiques ou des Poteries Considerérées dans Leur Histoire, Leur Practique et Leur Théorie*), published in two volumes in 1844. Brongniart (1770–1847), amongst other things a chemist and a geologist, was appointed director of the porcelain manufactory at Sèvres in 1800, and carried out extensive chemical studies of the raw materials and products of Sèvres and its competitors until his death in 1847. Also known to Shaw was that Brongniart aimed to create a museum at Sèvres with examples of ceramics from all over the world. To this end, Brongniart had written a letter dated 8 March 1836 to the editor of 'Silliman's Journal' (subsequently the *American Journal of Science and Arts*), with a request to acquire samples of North American pottery. This letter (Brongniart, 1837) states that the objective of creating such a museum was to address the following questions:

i) What kinds of pottery are used by the different classes of inhabitants of the country: the agriculturists, the mechanics, citizens, and merchants, poor, and rich?
ii) Is the pottery of native or foreign manufacture?
iii) If foreign, from what country does it come, and in what way?
iv) If of native manufacture, where is it made?

Although explicitly not archaeological, it is clear from points (ii)–(iv) that the importance of identifying the origin of ceramics for interpreting social structures, and hence the fundamental idea of ceramic provenance, was already in circulation in the 1830s – before Göbel's archaeological exposition in 1842.

Ceramics are one of the most ubiquitous finds in archaeology, as a result of their extensive use in many archaeological cultures, and also of their relative stability in the burial environment. Functionally, they serve as everything from utilitarian cooking and storage vessels, transport vessels, high-quality domestic fine wares for dining on or simply for decoration, and prestige wares for elite display. They have often fulfilled a role in funerary rites, and for many years common typological and stylistic characteristics were used to define 'cultures' in prehistoric archaeology. Equally, before the advent of radiocarbon dating, stylistic analysis of pottery was the mainstay of creating archaeological chronologies – for example, in the Minoan and Mycenaean world, successive time periods are defined by pottery types.

Fundamentally, ceramics are made from clay, although in China many ceramics are actually made from crushed rock which is converted into clay. For all but the simplest of wares, the clay is carefully prepared before forming into a vessel. This might involve levigating the clay in water to remove coarse particles, and can include the mixing of clays from different sources to optimize the physical properties of the material. In some cases, temper can be added to the clay to give the finished product particular desired properties, such as thermal shock resistance (although, depending on the extent of the pre-treatment of the clay, there may be a certain amount of natural temper in the fabric). Tempers can range from crushed rock, calcareous materials such as shell, or even organic components such as straw. The prepared clay is formed into a vessel using one or more construction techniques such as coil building, slab building, or turning on a wheel. Once formed, the 'green' vessel is dried before firing. For some vessels, a glaze or gloss is applied to the surface consisting of a layer which is more readily vitrifiable than the body but which matches the thermal expansion properties of the base clay. Once prepared, the vessel is fired at high temperature to induce irreversible chemical changes in the body and surface. Firing can be in a bonfire, a simple kiln, or in an elaborately designed kiln, and typical temperatures can range from c. 800°C up to around 1,400°C. As well as temperature, an important factor in the firing process is the availability of oxygen in the kiln (the redox conditions). Reducing conditions are a consequence of restricted oxygen availability, and oxidizing occurs when oxygen is freely available. The final appearance of the wares, and hence the success of the firing, is highly dependent on the control of the firing conditions over the extended period of firing. This can involve systematically changing the temperature and redox conditions over the period of the firing, which places major demands on the design of the kiln. General texts covering the various aspects of studying archaeological pottery include Shepard (1956), Olin and Franklin (1982), Rice (1987), Freestone and Gaimster (1997), Orton and Hughes (2013), and Hunt (2017).

From this, it is clear that ceramics are potentially complex materials which may or may not have a direct chemical relationship with a single geological source. On the other hand, it might be thought that recycling of ceramics is rare, making the material more suitable for study than, say, metals or glass, where recycling is possible or even probable. The most common form of ceramic recycling is repurposing, such as the reuse of transport amphorae as storage vessels, or the use of broken ceramics as building material as seen in Pompeii (Duckworth and Wilson, 2020). More prosaically, broken vessels can be used to render boggy ground more passable for humans, vehicles, and animals. None of these carry implications for provenance, but one practice which might impact is the grinding up of used pottery to form 'grog', added as temper to new vessels, which might have symbolic as well as physical meaning – emphasizing continuity of links with ancestors or relatives. We should, therefore, exercise a little caution when assuming that the recycling of ceramics is of little consequence to provenance studies. In China, Wang Zongmu (王宗沐), writing in the *Jiangxisheng dazhi* (江西省大志: *The great gazette of Jiangxi province*) in 1597, gives six recipes for ceramic body production of Imperial wares at the Jingdezhen official kiln. The recipes vary according to the size of the vessel (pp. 820–821; 836–839), but all include the addition of 'scrapings of unfired body material' at around 10–15% by weight. These scrapings are the unused body material from throwing and decorating the vessels, which often would involve a lot of turning to reduce thickness. This unfired but dried clay was obviously returned to the potters for recycling into the next batch of production. If all the clay is the same, then such recycling is unlikely to affect the chemical composition very much, but if several body types or grades are being made in the same workshop, then there is potential for some cross-contamination of sources.

The presence of grog is usually most easily seen by visual examination of the fabric on a broken edge. The first step in any scientific analysis of ceramics is always a visual examination of the fabric, often followed by closer study with low-power magnification, and then sometimes a high-magnification study of prepared thin sections, either under polarized light or at even higher magnification in the electron microscope. The first optical study of thin sections, called ceramic petrology, is credited to Anna O. Shepherd (1903–1971) in her work on Pecos pottery from the US Southwest published in 1936. For some pottery, petrography is often the only scientific study required to provenance the wares. An experienced eye can usually identify the nature of the clay and the added temper, leading to matching different groups of pottery, and deducing (or at least constraining) where they might have been made. Furthermore, such observation allows the interpretation of how a pot was created and fired, giving information on ceramic technology. Usually, all types of pottery can benefit from both optical and chemical studies, but, crudely speaking, coarse wares are more likely to benefit from optical study, whereas finewares and high fired ceramics (porcelain) are more likely to yield results from chemical analysis.

Despite these potential issues, ceramics have been an extremely attractive target for chemical provenance studies. For vessels which are extensively traded (e.g., transport vessels such as amphorae, or highly desirable finewares), tracing the vessels back to manufacturing source can be direct evidence for such trade and therefore a proxy for economic analysis, and have been extensively studied scientifically since the 1950s. Although ceramics were analysed early on in the history of chemistry (e.g., Vauquelin, 1800), and were extensively studied at the great porcelain factories for commercial purposes (e.g., Brongniart (1844) at Sèvres), it has been suggested that the first analysis of archaeological ceramics was that of Theodore William Richards of Harvard University (1868–1928: the first American scientist to be awarded a Nobel Prize, but not for his archaeological research) in the *American Chemical Journal* of 1895, in which he gives the complete composition of a vase fragment from Athens in the Boston Museum of Fine Arts. This assertion of primacy is not completely true, since earlier scholars had analysed various Egyptian, classical, and Chinese vessels (Pollard, 2015), but it does signify the beginnings of the serious chemical study of archaeological ceramics, and in particular of Mediterranean ceramics. The first published spectrometric analysis of archaeological ceramics was that of Eva Richards in 1959, at the Research Laboratory for Archaeology and the History of Art, University of Oxford, on 11 Romano-British mortaria. Following encouragement from Sinclair Hood (1917–2021), then the Director of the British School at Athens, the Oxford lab subsequently became involved in several large-scale studies of the provenance of Bronze Age Greek ceramics, coordinated by Hector Catling (1924–2013), at that time Assistant Keeper of Antiquities at the Ashmolean Museum, with the analyses done by Eva Richards, Ann Millett, and Audrey Blin-Stoyle (Catling *et al.*, 1961, 1963; Catling and Millett, 1965a, 1965b, 1966, 1969; Millett and Catling, 1967). This partnership between Oxford and the British School at Athens was to continue for the next 25 years, culminating in the publication of *Greek and Cypriote Pottery – A Review of Scientific Studies* by Richard Jones in 1986. Initially the work was carried out by optical emission spectrometry, but this was replaced in the

1970s by atomic absorption spectrometry. These techniques principally measure major and minor oxides in the ceramics (originally Al_2O_3, Na_2O, MgO, CaO, Fe_2O_3, TiO_2, MnO_2, Cr_2O_3, and NiO: K_2O was subsequently added; SiO_2, if reported, was usually estimated by difference, but occasionally measured directly). The original aim was to 'establish whether the chemical constituents of the clays used by potters of the Late Bronze Age at sites throughout Crete, Greece and the Greek Islands differ significantly from site to site or region to region, to the point where such differences can be used to identify the sources of manufacture of controversial vases and fragments' (Catling *et al.*, 1961: 31–32). An important aspect of this was distinguishing between vessels made on Crete (Minoan) and those from mainland Greece (Mycenaean) following the assumed conquest of the palace at Knossos on Crete by Mycenaeans (conventionally dated to c. 1450 BCE), and the subsequent merging of pottery styles. The early results were encouraging: using test samples of 40 from both Knossos and Mycenae, it was shown that the ranges of Mg and Cr did not overlap at all. Expanding the analyses to more than 200 sherds showed that the Mycenaean-style samples from the mainland sites of Berbati, Megara Minoa, and Korakou, and several sites on Cyprus, all appeared to match the Mycenaean control sherds. With the caveat that more sites needed to be studied, the discrimination between Mycenaean and Minoan pottery was deemed a success.

As with many things in archaeological science, more work often leads to the emergence of a more complicated picture. By 1965, the number of pottery 'types' (i.e., compositional groups) from the Bronze Age Aegean stood at 15, labelled A to O. Some were specific to particular sites, but others, such as Type A corresponding to the Peloponnese, and Type B to Minoan sites, were more regional. In this context, a very significant archaeological problem was addressed – the origin of the Inscribed Stirrup Jars found at Thebes (Catling and Millett, 1965a). This concerned a group of 80 Stirrup Jars found in the Mycenaean Palace at Thebes in Boeotia (Central Greece), around 30 of which carried inscriptions in Linear B, an early Greek script assumed to have originated in Crete at Knossos. At the time, Linear B in Crete was restricted to Knossos itself, although the preceding (undeciphered) script Linear A was widely used throughout Crete. Linear B inscriptions were known from other sites in mainland Greece (including Mycenae itself, and Pylos), but were dated to approximately 200 years after the destruction of Knossos. The key question, therefore, was whether these Theban jars were locally made or were, as widely presumed, imported from Crete. In principle, the recently developed chemical discrimination technique, already described, should provide a simple solution. However, analysis of 25 of these sherds produced the unexpected result of a range of potential sources, including eastern Crete, but not Knossos – which contradicted the archaeological evidence for the distribution of Linear B script. As noted by the authors (Catling and Millett, 1965a: 32): 'nobody will be pleased with the outcome'. However, an interesting additional observation had been made in the course of the work, and is purely attributable to the fact that the analytical technique used – optical emission spectroscopy with photographic plate detection – records all the emission lines from the sample, not just those of the elements being looked for. Re-examination of the original photographic plates showed that the two otherwise indistinguishable sources of Thebes and Crete could be discriminated by the levels of germanium (Ge) in the samples. This was not, however, sufficient to defend the work from criticism. In particular, Raison (1968) called into question not only the results on the Theban Stirrup Jars but also indirectly the whole concept of determining ceramic provenance by chemical analysis. A full rebuttal was published by Catling and Millett (1969), but doubts remained in some circles. A re-analysis of some of the samples, carried out at the Marc and Ismene Fitch Laboratory at the British School at Athens (Catling and Jones, 1977), came up with a slightly different result, simply because by that time more control samples had become available from Chania, in western Crete, and the Theban Stirrup Jars were eventually assigned to west Crete – a result deemed more archaeologically acceptable, in the light of the subsequent finding of similar Inscribed Stirrup Jars at Chania.

This slightly convoluted saga of the study of Inscribed Stirrup Jars is highly instructive, and illustrates the iterative nature of approaching the truth in archaeological science. It is undoubtedly the case in this example that the first publications came to the wrong conclusion, largely because insufficient comparative data were available. Interestingly, had the first analyses come up with a 'satisfactory' conclusion (i.e., coherent results, all pointing to either local Theban or imported Knossian origins), it is unlikely that further work would have been carried out, and these (incorrect) results would by now have become entrenched in the literature. A larger database, and a number of critical comments (including Raison, 1968; Wilson, 1976; McArthur, 1978), some more constructive than others, pushed the original authors to extend and improve their work for more than 10 years. In addition to a vast increase in the number of samples analysed, the reproducibility of the analyses was re-evaluated, leading to the adoption of internationally agreed pottery standards to be included in all publications, which in turn made the possibility of large databases containing results from multiple laboratories more realizable. The initial reliance on nine oxides (Al_2O_3, Na_2O, MgO, CaO, Fe_2O_3, TiO_2, MnO_2, Cr_2O_3, and NiO) for all potential sources was seen as too inflexible, and encouraged consideration of other elements depending on the specific geological contexts. Moreover, the original data analysis was effectively by eye, although various graphical presentations were used in an attempt to reflect confidence levels of group concentrations. By the late 1970s, the increased availability of mainframe computers, or even desktop versions, allowed much greater access to numerical multivariate techniques. In his synthetic publication of the results and data from more than 20 years of chemical work carried out on Aegean ceramics in Oxford and Athens, Jones (1986) presented the chemical results on approximately 4,277 samples, as well as offering extensive interpretations on the implications of these data, including the conclusion that the most likely source of the Stirrup Jars inscribed with Linear B script is Chania (Jones, 1986: 477–494).

Should Catling and Millett have refrained from publishing their first set of results in 1961, given it is now apparent that the then existing comparative database was inadequate? Of course, in an ideal world, they should have, but it took more than 10 years to get to a solution which was consistent archaeologically and philologically. If they had not published, and dealt seriously with the concerns raised, the work probably would not have advanced in the same way. This suggests that we should accept an iterative approach, where publication of preliminary results, followed by constructive criticism and self-reflection, helps in our approach towards the truth.

In parallel with this work in Europe, a different approach began in North America using NAA, which led to a number of large-scale analytical provenance studies. Around Christmas 1954, J. R. Oppenheimer (1904–1967), Director of the Institute for Advanced Study at Princeton, sent a letter to R. W. Dodson, Chairman of the Chemistry Department at Brookhaven National Laboratory, Long Island, NY, suggesting the possible use of trace element analysis by NAA as a means of characterizing archaeological pottery, and asking his opinion on the feasibility of this (Harbottle and Holmes, 2007). According to Sayre and Dodson (1957), this was followed by a meeting: ‘On March 31, 1956, at the invitation of Dr. Robert Oppenheimer, a group of archaeologists and chemists met at the Institute for Advanced Study to discuss the possibility of applying the methods of nuclear research to the study of archaeology.’ From this pilot study of 18 ceramic samples from around the Mediterranean (six terracotta figurines from Tarsus, two amphorae handles (from Rhodes and Pergamon), two pottery fragments from Boeotia, and eight sherds of Arretine ware from Arezzo) carried out at the Brookhaven National Laboratory, Long Island, NY, were born several large research programmes at Brookhaven and elsewhere, which ran for the next 50 years and more. Quantification in this first attempt was based on a comparison of the decay curves of induced gamma activity, particularly the ratio of Mn to Na, in each sample. Technological improvements, particularly the development of lithium-drifted germanium (Ge(Li)) detectors, gave much better resolution across the range of gamma ray energies, and quickly allowed more than 30 elements to be accurately and precisely quantified, to the point where, by the end of the 20th century, NAA had become the 'industry standard' for chemical analysis across a wide range of scientific fields, including archaeology (Glascock and Neff, 2003).

Perhaps the longest-running and most distinctive project carried out at Brookhaven was the 'Fine Paste Ceramics Project', which started in 1965 and ran for the next 50 years under the charismatic guidance of Edward V. Sayre (1919–2007) and Garman Harbottle (1923–2016) (Bishop, 2003; Harbottle and Holmes, 2007). The ceramics in question were several groups of fine Maya ceramics with orange paste from southern Mesoamerica, dating to the Terminal Classic period (c. 800–900 CE). The initial hypothesis was that there was a single production site for Maya Fine Orange, and the aim was to locate this area. On the basis of about 150 samples, it was proposed that there was a major compositional difference between Fine Orange and Fine Gray ceramics from the Maya area and those from the Veracruz-Oaxaca regions. Within the Maya area, the major locus of Fine Orange and Fine Gray production was found to be the Usumacinta river valley in southern Mexico and Guatemala, but 'micro-compositional differences' within ceramics from the Usumacinta drainage area were taken to argue against trade from a single production centre (Sabloff, 1982). In his extremely thoughtful review of the application of scientific approaches to the understanding of the Mesoamerican economy, Bishop (2014) concludes that 'these data served as the basis for many models of long-distance exchange as a means of explaining the development of cultural complexity', but noted that 'compositional data is now more directed toward localized investigations of economic activity'. The inference to be taken from this observation is perhaps that large-scale projects, involving numerous archaeologists, across many sites, and requiring many objects to be analysed, are increasingly difficult to sustain because of a lack of resources and analytical facilities.

Neutron activation analysis was rapidly taken up elsewhere as an analytical archaeological tool. Almost contemporaneously with Sayre's work at Brookhaven, Vera Emeleus in Oxford, using the reactor at Harwell, carried out studies on ceramics and coins (Emeleus, 1958, 1959, 1960; Emeleus and Simpson, 1960). Between the early 1960s and 1980s, a number of nuclear reactor facilities began programmes of archaeological analysis, primarily ceramics, including the Lawrence Berkeley National Laboratory in California, University of Michigan, the Smithsonian Museum and National Institute of Standards (NIST) in Washington DC, University of Missouri, University of Toronto, University of Manchester, the Hebrew University of Jerusalem, University of Bonn, Budapest, and so on. Most of these, with the exception of MURR and Bonn, which still have an Archaeometry laboratory, have now ceased operation (Boulanger, 2017).

In 1982, Garman Harbottle estimated that there had been 50,000 analyses of archaeological ceramics worldwide (Harbottle, 1982). Perhaps the most significant ceramic contribution came from the Lawrence Berkeley National Laboratory (LBNL) in California, first reported by Isadore Perlman (1915–1991) and Frank Asaro (1927–2014) in 1967. By 1969, they reported the analyses of more than 1,000 sherds or pottery from around the eastern Mediterranean, quantifying up to 38 elements, with a special interest in 2nd millennium BCE Cypriote pottery. They also produced a standard ceramic material ('Standard Pottery') which became widely used by all laboratories carrying out work on Mediterranean ceramics. The history of the LBNL activities in nuclear archaeology was discussed in Asaro and Adan-Bayewitz (2007). Between LBNL and the Hebrew University of Jerusalem (to where Perlman went after retiring from Berkeley) many thousands of samples have been analysed. On Asaro's retirement from LBNL, the ceramic database was donated to MURR – the University of Missouri Research Reactor Archaeometry Laboratory. In 2007, about 8,000 of these data were digitized (Boulanger, 2012) and are now available through the Digital Archaeological Record (www.tdar.org/), along with much supporting archaeological data. Data from more than 300 internal archaeological projects are also available at the MURR archaeological database (https://archaeometry.missouri.edu/murr_database.html), plus external data including the LBNL, Smithsonian/NIST, and University of Manchester databases. The Bonn Archaeometry Database (https://mommsen.hiskp.uni-bonn.de/datas.html) contains numerous NAA ceramic analyses, mostly from the Mediterranean, and their research programme is ongoing.

The paper by Asaro and Adan-Bayewitz (2007: 202), summarizing the history of the LBNL ceramic analysis programme, begins with an interesting and important remark. Commenting on the provenance work being carried out in Oxford by Catling and his colleagues in the 1960s, Perlman and Asaro are quoted as follows:

> They liked the sample selection procedures, but believed that the wrong technique – emission spectroscopy (ES) – was being used to measure element abundances. Perlman and F.A. thought that much better measurement precision could be achieved with INAA than with emission spectroscopy, and a larger suite of elements could be measured. Consequently, it would be possible, they thought, to assign the pottery samples to different areas of the Peloponnese, which Catling *et al.* (1963) could not do using ES.

Was emission spectroscopy the 'wrong technique' for provenance work on ceramics? The debate is essentially one between the use of analytical techniques capable of producing major and minor oxide compositions, but with limited sensitivity to trace elements, compared to those techniques producing a suite of trace element data, but not necessarily quantifying all the major and minor oxides. Many would say 'yes' – the analytical precision of NAA for most elements is much better than the equivalent for OES, and the number of elements measurable is in practice much greater. The compilation of large databases from several laboratories was facilitated by interlaboratory comparisons on standard materials, and sophisticated multivariate techniques became available to produce meaningful archaeological groupings from such highly dimensioned data. However, others would say that OES data, and its successor major element techniques, such as XRF and SEM, has its place. In concentrating on major and minor oxides in the ceramic matrix, in addition to providing the possibility of provenance, it allows a more direct relationship to be built between chemical composition, raw material use, and ceramic technology. It might be fair to say that if the objective is *purely* to provenance ceramics, then NAA provides the most reliable technique. If, however, the aim is to combine provenance with technological studies in terms of *chaîne opératoire*, then OES (and its successors such as AAS and XRF) might be more suitable (see, for example, the reconstruction of the raw material mineralogy of Chinese porcelain from AAS data in Pollard and Wood (1986)). In most senses, however, this debate has been rendered obsolete by the development of inductively coupled plasma techniques of analysis, since they can measure most major and minor elements, plus a large suite of trace elements. The capacity to carry out NAA analyses has declined dramatically in the 21st century, largely because many research reactors have been closed. NAA continues at some centres, and continues to be promoted by some (e.g., Riehle *et al.*, 2023), but the majority of analysts have switched to ICP-OES and ICP-MS.

6.3 Glass

Glass in this context is defined as an artificial vitrified product, made from sand or crushed quartz (silica) and an alkali source (plant ash or mineral), potentially with added stabilizers, colorants, decolourizers, or opacifiers. The earliest glass vessels date from the mid 2nd millennium BCE, in either Egypt or Mesopotamia, or both, but earlier vitreous materials exist, including glazed stones and faience. Faience is a synthetic material consisting of partially sintered coarse silica grains, often with a glazed surface, which is perhaps the earliest known artificial material, and not to be confused with the term faience used in the context of soft paste porcelain.

Glasses and glazed surfaces are in the vitreous state, which means that within certain parameters they have no fixed composition or physical properties such as melting point (Pollard *et al.*, 2017: 188–202). The earliest glasses are brightly coloured using a wide range of mineral colouring agents, prompting the thought that they may have been seen as 'simulated gemstones' (Shortland, 2012).

Egyptian faience has been the subject of chemical analysis since the late 19th century (Hoffman, 1885), and particularly by Alfred Lucas (1867–1945), who became Director and Principal Chemist of the Government Analytical Laboratory in Cairo, resulting in his influential publication *Ancient Egyptian Materials and Industries* (Lucas, 1926). He was also the chief chemist and conservator associated with the excavation of the tomb of Tutankhamun. Interest in provenance studies of faience beads began with Beck and Stone (1936), who studied the Bronze Age beads of the British Isles, and concluded from an archaeological analysis (supplemented by observations on specific gravity) that they probably originated in Egypt. This was followed up by a spectroscopic study by Stone and Thomas (1956), who reported semi-quantitative data on 15 elements from 136 faience beads from the UK, Europe, and Egypt. The initial expectation was that, from earlier work, 'clear trends in the composition of faience beads would be found which could be correlated with both source and date of manufacture' (Stone and Thomas, 1956: 75). Perhaps unsurprisingly given the rather coarse quality of the data, the conclusion was that 'spectrographic analysis of faience beads does not provide any unequivocal indication of their source or date of origin' (Stone and Thomas, 1956: 77). More detailed analysis using fully quantitative NAA of 22 elements (Aspinall *et al.*, 1972) suggested that British beads were characterized by having a higher tin content than Egyptian, Mediterranean, and other European beads, suggesting independent production rather than importation from Egypt. It was subsequently emphasized using the same data (Harding and Warren, 1973) that Eastern European beads were also chemically distinct, urging scholars to cease 'describing them as imports from Egypt or the Near East unless they find new and compelling evidence for doing so'.

Although faience appeared in the 5th millennium BCE, glass vessels did not occur until the mid 2nd millennium BCE, approximately simultaneously in Egypt and Mesopotamia, although the current opinion is that the first production on any scale was in Mesopotamia (Shortland, 2012: 47). Initially the vessels were made by coiling multicoloured strips of glass around a core, but by the 1st century BCE in the Roman Eastern Mediterranean glass blowing and moulding had allowed mass production (Fleming, 1999). The first reported quantitative analysis of archaeological glass (in fact, of glass of any kind: Caley, 1962: 13) was that of Klaproth (1798), who gave the detailed results on three pieces of coloured glass from the Villa of Tiberius on the

Italian island of Capri. In contrast to the picture for metal analysis, the growth in the number of analyses of glass was relatively slow, perhaps because of the more complex nature of the required gravimetric analysis (including more difficult dissolution protocols, and the need for the quantification of a greater number of elements (oxides)). The first publication of the analyses of a significant number of glasses (Egyptian, Mesopotamian, and Roman) was a series of papers by Neumann (1925, 1927, 1928, 1929), which reported about 62 gravimetric analyses, mostly carried out by his female assistants H. Hoffman, G. Kotyga, and M. Rupprecht. Purely in terms of numbers of analyses, this is to be compared with the publication in 1869 of 1,250 analyses of archaeological bronzes by von Bibra, showing the overwhelming focus on metal at the time. The first spectroscopic analyses of glass soon followed, which considerably increased the size of the dataset (initially approximately 200 analyses: Seligman *et al.*, 1936; Ritchie, 1936; Farnsworth and Ritchie, 1937; Seligman and Beck, 1938), the geographical scope of the glasses (China and Central Asia), and reduced the sample size required (to as little as 0.005 g), but the earliest data were semi-quantitative, reporting 20 elements on a complicated scale, subsequently converted to 0–5 by Caley (1962; 39–48). It was not until 1954 that fully quantitative data were produced by spectroscopy (Hahn-Weinheimer, 1954). She published quantified data for CuO, PbO, SnO_2, Sb_2O_3, and P_2O_5 for 44 samples of Roman window glass from across northern Europe, with the express purpose of determining the sources of the raw materials used – the first specific expression of provenance for glass.

By the Roman period, glass was widely traded, and potentially therefore an important indicator of economics and commerce across the empire and further afield. However, attempts to determine provenance by trace elements were broadly unsuccessful. This was probably due to several factors, amongst which is the chemical complexity of glass. Historically, it is composed from silica – either sand or crushed quartz – modified by a source of alkali to reduce the working temperature, and often a stabilizer containing calcium (Pollard *et al.*, 2017: 195–200). The alkali can be provided from a mineral source such as natron, which is a natural evaporite mineral of variable chemical composition, or by ash from various types from burnt plants. These can either be sodium-rich if the plants are halophytes such as glasswort (of genus *Salicornia*) or, as described by Theophilus (Hawthorne and Smith, 1963), from beech leaves, rich in potassium. The stabilizer could be provided by shells naturally intermixed with the source of sand, or as a specific calcareous mineral. In terms of provenance, this means that the trace elements in the glass can be associated with either the silica sources or with the alkali and/or stabilizer sources.

Furthermore, glass can either be colourless (transparent) or brightly coloured by the addition of small amounts of particular minerals – typically copper for pale blues, cobalt for dark blues, lead and tin or antimony for yellow, and iron for dark colours. Transparency can be enhanced by the addition of decolourizers such as manganese to remove the typical pale-green colour of glass made from less pure sands. When all of this is combined with the potential for contamination from the crucible and furnace linings during melting, and also the possibility of old glass being used as a contribution to the furnace charge (cullet), it is clear that the trace elements are unlikely to provide a direct link with specific sources. Subsequent work has also pointed to an important technological distinction – that between primary and secondary glass production. Primary production is where the raw materials – silica, alkali, cullet, and so on – are melted together to form raw glass. Secondary production is where raw glass is converted to finished products such as vessels, and possibly where coloured glasses are manufactured. At least for the Roman period, it is likely that primary production took place at a very few places, primarily around the Mediterranean, whereas secondary production occurred at many places around the empire (Foy *et al.*, 2000; Degryse, 2014). There is limited evidence for primary glass production at provincial sites such as York (Jackson *et al.*, 1998), but it is likely that most raw glass was produced at a limited number of Mediterranean sources, and subsequently transported for further processing, probably by sea or river. The trace element patterns observed in glass are therefore determined initially by the site of primary production, but potentially modified by secondary production, to the point where distinct clustering of data may represent particular batches of secondary production (e.g., Foster and Jackson, 2010).

Given this complexity, it is not surprising that analysts sought to expand the portfolio of data on glass by adding isotopic measurements (Degryse, 2013), and also to target elements which are primarily associated with the sand sources. As already noted, glass was, along with lead, the first archaeological material to be subjected to lead isotope analysis (Brill and Wampler, 1967a; 1967b), with oxygen isotopes being added by 1970 (Brill, 1970). This pioneering work was sufficient to demonstrate that both isotopes, especially when combined, can discriminate between glass from different sources, but the laborious chemical process needed to separate the lead for the measurement technique of the time (thermal ionization mass spectrometry) meant that relatively few analyses became available before the end of the century. The pace of glass research quickened considerably in the 21st century, with the development of strontium isotope ($^{87}Sr/^{86}Sr$) measurements in glass (Freestone *et al.*, 2003), originally used archaeologically by Noël Gale (1931–2014) for the analysis of obsidian (Gale, 1981). In the context of glass, strontium is generally associated with calcium, added as a stabilizer in the glass network. If the calcium is in the form of shell, then the Sr isotope ratio is associated with the source of the marine sand. This was quickly combined with the measurement of neodymium isotopes ($^{143}Nd/^{144}Nd$: Degryse *et al.* 2009), which are associated with fine-grained marine sediments. It has been shown that the neodymium isotope ratio varies significantly around the eastern Mediterranean coast, as a result of fractionation in the fine sediments deposited in the sea by the river Nile (Brems *et al.*, 2013). The combination of strontium and neodymium isotopes has worked well to identify the sources of glass-making sands around the Mediterranean (Degryse *et al.*, 2009).

The measurement of the heavy element isotope ratios in glass was aided considerably by the development of high-resolution multi-collector inductively coupled plasma mass spectrometry, which allowed rapid determination of a wide range of isotope ratios on either a solution containing minute amounts of sample or, using laser ablation, directly on the solid service. Most analysts prefer solution analysis because of the potential for isotopic fractionation during the laser ablation process (Zhang and Hu, 2020). Thus, Lobo *et al.* (2012, 2013, 2014) measured the antimony isotope ratio ($^{123}Sb/^{121}Sb$) in order to study the sources of antimony used in glass as either a decolourant or an opacifier. This work suggested that there were two isotopically distinct sources of antimony used in Roman glass, and that these sources were different from those used in Bronze Age Egypt and Mesopotamia. The sources, however, could not be uniquely identified by comparison with data from modern antimony deposits (Lobo *et al.*, 2013).

None of the discussed methods gives very much information about the source of the alkali used. A plot of $\%K_2O$ versus $\%MgO$ is traditionally used to distinguish between glasses made from plant ash and those using an evaporite mineral – in these diagrams, glass made from mineral sources of alkali fall in the region $K_2O < c.\ 1\%$, $MgO < c.1.2\%$, whereas plant ash glass tends to have both MgO and $K_2O > 2\%$ (Velde, 2013). Boron is a light element often associated with the alkali fluxes used to make the glass, and is rarely reported in chemical analyses because of difficulties in measuring such light elements. Devulder *et al.* (2013, 2014, 2015) have developed the measurement of boron isotopes ($^{11}B/^{10}B$) in archaeological glasses, and shown that not only can plant ash glasses be differentiated from natron (evaporate) glasses but also that the isotopic value of the boron can indicate specific geographical sources for the natron (Devulder *et al.*, 2014).

Undoubtedly, these developments, combined with more detailed trace element analyses such as the use rare earths and other transition metals (described on pp. 16–17), have resulted in a far better understanding of the provenance of glass, but one issue remains relatively intractable: the potential effect of mixing glasses from different sources. The distinction between primary and secondary sources of glass production, with the latter predominating at least in the Roman empire, means that substantial recycling is possible at these secondary sources. This could extend to the wholesale re-melting of glass to produce new vessels, perhaps at times when fresh glass from primary sources was less easily available, such as has been postulated for post-Roman Britain (Sainsbury, 2018). The use of minor contributions (perhaps 10% by weight) of recycled glass (cullet) in the melting furnace charge to reduce the necessity for fresh glass has been a common practice throughout history. Another potential use of recycled is the addition of small quantities of highly coloured glass as a 'pigment' when primary sources of mineral pigments are unavailable, such as the reuse of Roman dark blue (cobalt coloured) glass tesserae in the manufacture of dark blue glass in the post-Roman and even early Medieval period in northwest Europe, when it is believed that access to sources of cobalt minerals was restricted (Bidegaray and Pollard, 2018).

The availability of high-quality multi-element and isotopic data on glasses has made it possible to begin to address this issue. Degryse *et al.* (2006), adopting a technique developed in earth sciences (e.g., Faure, 1986: 142–147), have suggested the use of plots of inverse concentration of strontium against the strontium isotopic ratio (1/Sr versus $^{87}Sr/^{86}Sr$) as a useful tool for detecting mixing. Others have used trace element data, particularly focussing on those added elements designed to either colour of decolour glass, particularly the elements antimony and manganese (Silvestri *et al.*, 2008; Foster and Jackson, 2010). Contamination by iron in the primary sand usually gives an undesirable pale green or blue colour to transparent glass, so both these elements have been used at different times to counter these tints and produce truly transparent glass (Biron and Chopinet, 2012). On the assumption that glassmakers would not have taken the trouble to decolorize glass which was intended to be deeply coloured, the presence of either Sb or Mn (or both) at levels above background (a few tens of parts per million (ppm)) in coloured glasses is taken to suggest that mixing has taken place, via the introduction of decolorized glass into the melt. Similarly, if elements normally associated with colouring or opacifying glass, such as cobalt, copper, antimony, tin, or lead, are present above background levels in colourless glass, then it might be assumed that these have been introduced in small amounts of coloured glass added to the melt, albeit at levels which do not affect the final colourless nature of the glass. Careful measurements can even be used to constrain the estimate of the quantities of added glass.

6.4 Metals

The use of metal has been seen as one of the major technological achievements of human society – indeed, the presence of metal has been used as the key definition of two of the perceived phases of human development – the Bronze Age and the Iron Age. Although archaeological thinking has now moved beyond the simplistic assumption that these 'ages' were defined by the use of these metals, there is no doubt that metal, in the form of tools, weapons, vessels, statues, and generally as symbols of wealth and power, had an important impact on society. Because of this, the origins of metallurgy have been the subject of intense academic scrutiny for several centuries. It is assumed that native metal (e.g., gold, silver, copper) was the first to be exploited, as a consequence of humans searching for brightly coloured ores, for pigment and decoration. Starting perhaps in the 7th millennium BCE, and probably in or around Anatolia, the smelting of metal from ores, particularly copper, had spread across all of Eurasia by the 2nd millennium BCE (Roberts *et al.*, 2009). Metals, therefore, have occupied a central place in archaeological thinking, and inevitably became the focus of provenance studies at an early date.

Following the development of gravimetric analyses in the 18th and 19th centuries already discussed, the pace of analysis increased rapidly with the adoption of instrumental methods of analysis (initially optical emission spectroscopy, OES), in the 1920s. Several large European projects were initiated with the explicit aim of discovering the source of the copper used to make Bronze Age metal artefacts (Pernicka, 2014; Pollard *et al.*, 2018). In the UK, the British Association for the Advancement of Science (BAAS) established the 'Sumerian copper committee', led by Cecil Henry Desch (1874–1958), with the aim of reporting on 'the probable source of the supply of copper used by the Sumerians'. Between 1928 and 1938, the Committee reported nearly 200 analyses to the annual meeting of the BAAS. The analyses were carried out in the Metallurgical Department of the National Physical Laboratory, a government-funded laboratory at Teddington, Middlesex. Its successor after the war was the Ancient Mining and Metallurgy Committee of the Royal Anthropological Institute, established in 1945 (Anon., 1946). Like its predecessor, this Committee had the provenance of archaeological copper as its primary focus – '(t)he main question now before this committee is whether there are any means of recognizing the locality from which the metal in a given copper object was obtained' (Coghlan *et al.*, 1949: 6). Between 1948 and 1957, it published more than 20 papers focussing mostly on Eastern Europe and the Near East. This particular initiative was notable because it brought together some of the leading archaeologists of the day (e.g., V. Gordon Childe (1892–1957) and Christopher

Hawkes (1905–1992)) with some of the foremost metallurgists (e.g., Desch) and geologists (e.g., Cyril E. N. Bromehead (1885–1952)).

Several groups of researchers in the German-speaking world started large-scale analytical programmes of archaeological metals in the 1930s. The first significant compilation of OES data, and the largest published dataset since that of von Bibra (1869), came from the University of Halle, where Helmut Otto (1910–1998) and Wilhelm Witter (1866–1949) set out to understand the prehistoric metallurgy of Europe using chemical analysis, to replace the previous typological approaches. In 1952, they published *Handbuch der ältesten vorgeschichtlichen Metallurgie in Mitteleuropa* (Otto and Witter, 1952), containing the analyses of 1,374 European artefacts for the elements Fe, Co, Ni, Cu, As, Sn, Ag, Sb, Pb, Bi, and S by their own OES method, which involved converting about 0.2 g of metal from the sample into two electrodes through which a high voltage was passed. From visual observation, they divided the data into six groups: 'pure copper (Reinkupfer)', 'raw copper (rohkupfer)' (defined as 'copper with small traces of other elements'), 'arsenical copper alloy (arsen-kupferlegierung)', 'Fahlerzmetalle' (defined as 'copper with a higher percentage of trace elements than raw copper', divided into 'Fahlerz with a high percentage of silver' and 'Fahlerz with a low percentage of silver', 'other kinds of metal (sonstige metalle mit Ni, As und Ag)', and 'copper-tin alloy (zinn-kupferlegierung)'. They claimed that most of the German artefacts came from copper ores in Saxony, but this conclusion has subsequently been challenged (Pernicka, 2011: 28).

Another important group was established in Vienna in the 1930s, led by Richard Pittioni (1906–1985) and Ernst Preuschen (1898–1973), focussing on the Alpine and Balkans regions (Preuschen and Pittioni, 1937). They eschewed the methodology of Otto and Witter, believing that provenance could only be assigned after assembling a significant amount of data on specific forms of the same period (Pittioni, 1957: 3). Moreover, they said that it is impossible to determine the provenance of a single object because metal ores are too heterogeneous, and the ore composition is not the same at all depths within a deposit. Consequently, two objects with different compositions could derive from a single ore source (Pittioni, 1957: 4). Useful information could, however, be derived by the combination of specific elements, particularly Sb, As, Pb, Ni, Ag, Bi, and Sn (Pittioni, 1957: 7). A consequence of the idea that it was the combination of presence/absence of particular elements was the decision to report only semi-quantitative analysis, without numerical concentrations. Unfortunately, this means that their data, consisting of 6,000 analyses, cannot be used in subsequent research, although their pioneering approach to the study of ancient mining sites remains a significant contribution.

The largest of the European metal analysis projects was started in Stuttgart by a group of researchers led by Siegfried Junghans (1915–1999), Edward Sangmeister (1916–2016), and Manfred Schröder (1926–2009). The project was titled *Studien zu den Anfangen der Metallurgie*, universally abbreviated to 'the SAM project'. They published the first 1,000 results in 1960, added 9,000 more in 1968, and finally reached 22,000 in 1974 (Junghans *et al.*, 1960; 1968, 1974). Their aim was to study the origin and spread of copper and bronze in the entire European continent by examining the material itself, using optical emission spectroscopy and statistical analysis (Junghans *et al.*, 1968: 6). Fortunately, they followed the philosophy of Otto and Witter rather than that of Pittioni, and reported quantitative data on 11 elements (Sn, Pb, As, Sb, Ag, Ni, Bi, Au, Zn, Co, and Fe, with Cu calculated by difference of the sum from 100%). Also in contrast to the Vienna group, they decided to focus on the regional distribution of chemical groupings of the objects themselves, rather than attempt to link the data directly with ancient ore sources revealed by an extensive associated fieldwork programme. Of the elements measured, they felt that Bi, Sb, Ag, Ni, and As provided the best discrimination between the different types of copper (Junghans *et al.*, 1960: 57). Their statistician, Hans Klein, developed a method to create compositional groups within the data, which he called statistical frequency analysis. His aim was to generate groupings within which the distribution of each element could be represented by a normal (Gaussian) curve. As a result, the first publication (Junghans *et al.*, 1960: Tabelle 1, p. 210) proposed the existence of 12 metal groups, labelled A, B1, B2, C1, C2, C3, E00, E01, E10, E11, F1, and F2, defined by a decision tree based on the concentrations of these five elements. The subsequent publication (Junghans *et al.*, 1968: 13), as well as increasing the number of analyses, carried out a more sophisticated 'two dimensional' analysis, consisting of initially classifying the data according to the concentrations of *both* As and Sb (N = both nil, III = both As and Sb $\leq$ 0.025%, IV = As $\leq$ 0.025% and Sb $\leq$ 0.025%, and so on), followed by subdivision of these groups according to the concentrations Bi, Ni, and Ag. This resulted in 29 groups, which they regarded as a more refined version of the original 12 (Junghans *et al.*, 1968: 15). The main output was a series of maps of Europe, showing the distribution of each of the 29 groups.

The reception accorded to the results of the SAM project in the archaeological world was generally negative. According to James D. Muhly, a leading scholar of Mediterranean archaeology, 'the reaction to the SAM Project was uniformly negative, ... Archaeologists were sceptical of the SAM metal groupings chiefly because the different classes of metal were presented within the context of an outmoded diffusionist archaeology that was (unfairly) used to discredit the entire project' (Muhly, 1993). The perceived problems seemed to stem largely from the statistical methodology used. Waterbolk and Butler (1965: 230) stated that the Stuttgart team had 'thrown the analyses all into one pot, with the hope that mathematical means will bring them out of the pot again in a logical order'. The consequence of this lack of integration of the archaeological data associated with each object apart from country of origin (often incomplete, but including precise find location, date, typology, manufacturing technique, decorative features, and so on) was that some defined groups often contained objects of different type, date, and location, and some coherent collections of artefacts from a single archaeological context were allocated to different groups. These criticisms of the Stuttgart group's statistical methodology have been generally accepted, but attempts to improve on the interpretations, such as that proposed by Waterbolk and Butler (1965), have generally presented little improvement. However, this does not undermine the fundamental importance of the Stuttgart group's work. A critical point was their decision to adopt the quantitative analytical methodology used by Otto and Witter. For the European Bronze Age, these data remain the largest and most comprehensive dataset available, which subsequent workers have attempted to reinterpret and evaluate (e.g., Krause and Pernicka, 1996; Pollard *et al.*, 2018). The full SAM database was published electronically by Krause (2003).

Meanwhile, in the Union of Soviet Socialist Republics, a very large programme of metal analyses was also being carried out concerning the bronze artefacts from Eastern Europe, Central Asia, and across the Russian continent, including Siberia up to the Urals in the east. By the end of the 1950s dedicated archaeometallurgical laboratories had been founded in Baku (Azerbaijan), Tbilisi (Georgia), St Petersburg, and Moscow. Each of these produced substantial quantities of data and carried out important regional studies. A significant contribution, however, came with the foundation of a second laboratory in Moscow within the Institute of Archaeology of the Soviet Academy of Sciences under the direction of Boris Kolchin (Б.А. Колчин), and associated from its inception with the work of Evgenij Chernykh (Е.Н. Черных). The total number of samples analysed is said to be in excess of 70,000, but there is no synthetic publication of these data. His main volume in English – *Ancient Metallurgy in the USSR* (Chernykh, 1992) – explains the data in terms of 'Metallurgical Provinces' – networks of central production and exchange – but no data were given, and no explanation of the novel interpretational methodology used. It was unfairly criticized in some quarters as being merely a Russian version of the SAM project, but that is not so. The subtlety of the approach is only apparent from a detailed study of the original publications. Although provenance was at the centre of the endeavour, Chernykh did not assume that it was straightforward, either geologically or metallurgically. On detailed examination, far from being a Russian reflection of the SAM project, the approach is one which emerged from a comprehensive critique of the existing methodologies in European archaeometallurgy.

Bearing in mind both Biek's (1957) and Thompson's (1958) observations that there may not be a direct relationship between trace elements in ores and smelted metal, Chernykh made a thorough metallurgical literature review, including experimental studies of the preferential movement of elements between metal, slag, and vapour (Okunev, 1960). From this he established a baseline for the choice of discriminating elements (Chernkyh, 1966: 18–21): Sn, Pb, As, Sb, Bi, Ag, Au, Co, Ni, and Zn. He also established a coherent approach to the definition of the boundary between 'artificial' (i.e., deliberately created by human choice) and 'natural' alloys (those including alloying elements as a consequence of impurities present in the ores) – for example, at around 1% for tin. He also discussed key problems relating to the recycling of metal, including the differentiation of primary alloys and alloyed metal resulting from the re-melting of scrap bronze with clean metal, and the impact of oxidative loss of particular elements on the overall composition of the metallurgical group. On recycling, he concluded:

> One of the most complex and difficult tasks is the identification of secondary, mixed metal [within the system]. Such [metal] derives from the re-melting of broken artefacts, made from metal smelted from different ores . . . and containing a complex array of elements . . . derived from its [original components]. Evidently, in some archaeological cultures it is possible to identify such mixed groups . . . [but] the methodology by which to differentiate this metal is not entirely clear. (Chernykh, 1966: 20–21)

Equally important, but missed in the initial critiques of his methodology, was his integration of archaeological and chemical information within a standardized statistical approach, described most fully in his second thesis (Chernykh, 1970). He codified various levels of groupings, which could be independent of each other:

- Chemical – based on a characteristic suite of elements, defined through a combination of visual and chemical analyses, and deemed distinctive of a particular region, mineralogical formation, or mine
- Metallurgical – based on characteristic alloying components (e.g., Sn > 1%) and independent of chemical groups
- Typological – based on various characteristics and proportions within broad functional-stylistic groupings.

He assigned the composition of each object to a limited number of metallurgical (alloy recipes) and chemical groups (trace elements) on the basis of visual examination of the data, which are specific to each study area. Following this, he explicitly combined typological and chemical analysis, producing two sets of correlations between assemblages, one for typology (R) and one for chemistry (S). For typology, he defined a set of typological categories, and allocated every object in the assemblage to one of these categories, producing a numerical summary of how many objects belong to each category for each assemblage. He then compared assemblages on a pairwise basis using a mathematical formula (see Pollard *et al.*, 2018: 28–30). The chemical correlation (S) for the objects classified into chemical groups was calculated in the same way. A graphical correlation showed the relationship between one cultural assemblage and all the other assemblages in his analysis. This allows an evaluation of the relationship between cultural assemblages for both typological and chemical data. This approach forms the basis of his derivation of metallurgical provinces. To quote from the introduction in Kohl (2007: xx): 'Although many problems remain unresolved and many paradoxes raised by his work are difficult to ponder, it is impossible to overestimate Evgenij's incredible contribution to our overall understanding of Bronze Age Eurasia. In a sense, we all follow in his footsteps.'

Inspired by the early British and German projects, other European countries established similar regionally- or nationally focussed metallurgical projects, such as Oldeberg (1942) in Sweden, who assembled 641 Swedish analyses, plus 45 from Norway, 47 from Denmark, and 13 from Finland. In France, Briard and Giot (1956) began by publishing 37 analyses on Breton metal, followed by Briard and Maréchal (1958) (53 analyses), and ultimately a set of four volumes entitled *Analyses spectrographiques d'objets préhistoriques et antiques* (Giot *et al.*, 1966, 1970, 1975, 1979), which contained 3,620 analyses. Large-scale analyses of bronzes came relatively late to China, despite the fact that the production of bronze in the Chinese Bronze Age was probably on a scale unseen in Europe until the classical period. Although some of the earliest European chemical analyses of metal were carried out on imported Chinese alloys (see p. 8), only a few groups of Chinese bronzes were analysed in the 19th century, and the earliest analyses to be carried out in East Asia date from the 1920s (Liu *et al.*, 2015). The first large-scale analyses were carried out at the Freer Gallery of Art in Washington DC, where more than 400 Shang and Zhou objects (mostly ritual vessels) from the Arthur M. Sackler collection of Chinese bronzes were analysed (Bagley, 1987; Rawson, 1990; So, 1995).

6.4.1 Lead Isotope Analysis

Following the initial development of lead isotope analysis in the 1960s (described in Section 5), and the first demonstration that isotopic measurements could be made on lead extracted from bronzes (Brill and Wampler, 1967b), attention initially switched to using the traces of lead in silver to provenance the silver (Gale and Stos-Gale, 1981a, 1981b; Stos-Gale and Gale, 1982). This was of particular interest to classical scholars, since it has been assumed that the wealth of ancient Athens was predicated on the control of the supply of silver from the nearby Laurion mines. Thus, determining the extent of the trade in Laurion silver was seen as a proxy for the extent of Athenian commerce.

At about the same time, it became apparent that the dissatisfaction with the results of the SAM project, and a lack of knowledge of Chernykh's work, resulted in most European and American archaeologists losing faith in the proposal that archaeological bronzes could be provenanced by chemical analysis. When it was shown that traces of lead in copper artefacts could be extracted and measured isotopically (Gale and Stos-Gale, 1982), the use of lead isotopes to identify the provenance of the copper was enthusiastically seized on as a potential solution. During the 1980s and 1990s, the lead isotope work on the metal supply in the Mediterranean was largely carried out by three laboratories: one in Oxford led by Noel Gale (1931–2014), one in Heidelberg led by Ernst Pernicka, and one in Washington led by Ed Sayre (1919–2007). This work has been extensively reviewed and summarized (Gale, 1991; Gale and Stos-Gale, 1992; Knapp and Cherry, 1994; Pollard *et al.*, 2017: 406–414). It generated praise and scepticism in equal measure, and descended into a rather acrimonious debate focussing not on the veracity of the measurements, but largely on how such data should be interpreted in archaeological terms (see, for example, a series of papers in the journal *Archaeometry* between 1992 and 1995). Whilst this debate had the effect of limiting the reliance that many Mediterranean archaeologists were prepared to put in the results, it is noteworthy that elsewhere in the world lead isotope studies on various materials were carried out successfully, and with considerable efficacy. In many ways, the situation was resolved by a change in instrumentation. The early work was carried out by thermal ionization mass spectrometry, which required specialized clean laboratories and instrumentation, and the number of labs interested in purely archaeological work was consequently very limited. Although no less demanding, the replacement of this technique by inductively coupled plasma mass spectrometry meant that many more laboratories were capable of measuring lead isotopes in archaeological material, and the method has now found wide acceptance as a powerful method for archaeological research.

7 Cracks in the Façade

Concerns about the veracity of scientific approaches to the provenance of archaeological materials have come essentially from two directions: one archaeological and one theoretical. Even from the inception of large-scale approaches to provenance in the mid 20th century, some archaeologists have expressed the view that the results of such studies were either ambiguous and unhelpful, or, in some cases, simply wrong. Such views, examples of which have already been given, were usually based on the lack of consistency between 'scientific' approaches and other sources of archaeological evidence, and prompted fierce debates about the role of science in archaeology (e.g., Dunnell, 1993). These criticisms were often well-founded, based on aspects of the methodologies employed, such as the adequacy of the sampling of archaeological objects and prospective sources of raw materials, but also on the interpretative frameworks employed. As the size of the datasets increased (both in terms of numbers of samples, but also in the range of characteristics measured), ever more complex mathematical approaches have been applied. Although theoretically justifiable (except it must be remembered that most multivariate approaches are empirically rather than statistically based), the increasing abstraction of the results simply contributed to the growing unease about the validity of these approaches.

The second strand of concern arose from theoretical issues about the nature of the processing of the materials being studied, and the relative lack of consideration of the articulation between material culture and human behaviour (Pollard and Gosden, 2023). The fundamental concept of scientific provenance – that the object carries within it some 'fingerprint' of the raw materials from whence it came – has been elaborated upon but not fundamentally reconsidered since the mid 19th century. It has, however, become increasingly obvious to many researchers that the production and circulation systems of many classes of object are potentially far more complicated than this simple postulate would suggest. Such factors include the following:

i) Theoretical consideration of time in the transport of objects
ii) The consequences of raw materials processing
iii) The effects of high temperature processing
iv) The effects of mixing and recycling

7.1 Time and Transport

Most models of trade and exchange in antiquity, such as shown in Figure 1, essentially assume that transport is instantaneous. This is reasonable in most cases – if not 'instantaneous', transport may only have taken a few days or months – possibly many months in the case of long-distance transport – but essentially instantaneous in terms of the time intervals we can detect archaeologically. This is particularly likely to be the case for large-scale highly organized and centralized systems such as the ancient empires of Rome, China, Egypt, and Mesopotamia, especially in the context of mass-produced items and their raw materials. However, in less centralized systems, such as those in regions outside these empires for much of prehistory, time may be a factor, especially if combined with intermittent down-the-line trading. Pollard *et al.* (2015) suggested that if an object (such as a copper axe) passed through several hands on its journey, and especially if it was temporarily retained and possibly reshaped at its intervening stops, then by the time it reaches its 'final' destination it could have been several decades (or possibly even centuries) old, and lost any distinctive visual characteristics of the place from whence it came. Thus, seen from the perspective of those at the end of this chain, it may simply have come from people across the nearest river or mountain. Although, scientifically speaking, it may be possible to show that it contains metal from a particular place, this may be archaeologically irrelevant. Even though the material itself can be shown to have moved from A to B, it might not signify any knowledge of, or connection between, place A on the part of the people at B. Thus, although the postulate of provenance may have been correctly applied, the consequential archaeological inference is completely untrue.

7.2 Raw Materials Processing

With the exception of lithic materials and obsidian, it is likely to be vanishingly rare for a raw material to be extracted from the ground and converted into an object with no further physical manipulation. Some simple ceramic objects may be made directly from a lump of good quality clay dug out of the ground, but mostly, as already noted, clays are crushed and picked to remove stones, washed, levigated, mixed together, and tempered to give the correct properties for the objects being produced. Glass is a complex material, requiring a source of silica, alkali, and modifier – each of which is likely to be processed to refine the material before mixing.

Metallic ores are inevitably processed before smelting – crushed, picked, sieved, roasted if necessary, and possibly blended to give the right charge for the furnace, which might also need other materials adding to promote slagging. Even before smelting, therefore, ores of different grades (and possibly from different mines) might have been mixed together. This is graphically illustrated in a Qing dynasty text on copper mining from Yunnan, southwest

China, written in 1844 by Wu Qujin (吳其濬), entitled 滇南礦廠工器圖略 (*An Illustrated Account of the Mines and Smelters of Yunnan*) (Vogel, 2008). He identifies five different types of copper ore minerals, differentiated by colour and texture, and containing different proportions of copper. According to Wu Qujin, the smelters would blend richer and poorer ores to achieve a target of about 20% copper by weight in the furnace charge. He also gives six different smelting processes appropriate to each different type of ore. The significance of this is that the smelter exercises his expertise (for it was probably a male occupation) in grading ores by eye to produce the optimal charge for the furnace. This would have involved taking different minerals, which could at the least have come from different parts of the same mine, and might have come from different mines in the region, depending on the organization of the mining community. The product – the raw unrefined copper – is already therefore a mixture of copper from different sources. If, as is often the case, the refining process is carried out at a regional level, then ingots from different smelters are further mixed to produce the refined copper for export. Although this is a narrative from a remote corner of China in the mid 19th century, it almost certainly reflects age-old practices from across a much wider region of China, and potentially beyond.

7.3 High Temperature Processing

The production of most inorganic raw materials of antiquity inevitably involves processing at high temperatures at one or more points in the manufacturing cycle. On the face of it, lithics and obsidian are again the major exceptions, but even these may have been exposed to some heating, either from fire setting to fracture the rockface in the quarry or heating to aid flaking during working. The majority of materials, however, require high temperature processing – bonfire or kiln firing for ceramics, ranging from 800°C to 1,400°C; primary and secondary melting furnaces for glass, with temperatures around 900°C; smelting furnaces for metals with temperatures of around 1,100°C for copper, and possibly higher for iron, often followed by similar temperatures during casting or other working processes. For many materials, it is not only control over temperature that is necessary, but also control over oxygen availability during the firing, sometimes varied over the course of the firing cycle. Thus, smelting metals requires reduction, but refining needs oxydizing conditions. Similarly, the colour developed by pottery, glazes, and glasses depends critically on the redox conditions within the furnace. From a provenancing perspective, all of these processes are potential sources of induced variability to the elemental composition and, at least theoretically, to certain isotope ratios.

This problem of volatalization during the roasting of ores was eloquently described at an early stage in the work of the Ancient Mining and Metallurgy Committee of the Royal Anthropological Institute, successor to the British Association's programme for the study of the sources of Sumerian copper. F. C. Thompson, Professor of Metallurgy at the University of Manchester, wrote the following in the context of copper ores:

> Where arsenic and antimony are present, as is normally the case with such ores, special conditions obtain. . . . The proportion of these elements present in the ore which ultimately enters the metal depends, therefore, on the exact conditions under which the roasting is carried out. . . . There is, therefore, no direct correlation between the content of these impurities in the ore, which, it must not be forgotten, may itself vary considerably even over distances of only a few feet, and in the metal; and at any given mine the composition of the roast and hence of the metal produced may have varied almost from day to day. . . . This must not be taken to imply that the work being done in analysing metallic samples and ores is without real value. What is required is a more critical consideration of such results by those well versed in metallurgical knowledge. (Thompson, 1958: 4)

Many elements are volatile at high temperatures, and are thus in danger of being preferentially removed during a high temperature process. Although the exact mechanisms of volatilization can be complicated – perhaps involving only elemental volatilization, but more commonly requiring one or more oxidation steps – in practice the relative tendencies are well-known and can be predicted in some circumstances. Zinc, for example, is notoriously volatile, as is arsenic, whereas silver and nickel are relatively stable in copper alloys. These relative volatilities have been used to estimate the degree of recycling in copper alloys by comparing the trace element composition of an assemblage of objects with the same elements in the assumed starting material (Pollard *et al.*, 2018: 107–111). Clearly, however, this can only be applied to simple systems in which the starting material can be identified with some confidence, and the only mechanism of the loss of trace elements is volatalization. Such situations are likely to be very rare.

7.4 Mixing and Recycling

The issues of mixing and recycling in the context of copper alloys and glass (and to a lesser extent in ceramics) have already been discussed, and will not be repeated here. Recycling is also likely to be an issue in precious metals (especially gold and silver) – in fact, the pressures to recycle are probably even greater in these materials than in copper. The situation with iron is somewhat more complicated, in that iron can be physically reused by re-forging, re-sharpening, and, for example, welding new blades onto worn-down iron knives. The degree to which iron was recycled in the same way as copper – that is, by adding old metal to the melting of new alloys – is yet to be determined (Bentley *et al.*, 2023).

8 Towards a New Provenance Hypothesis

For copper alloys, the potential for, if not the inevitably of, recycling has prompted a theoretical rethink about the nature of archaeological copper objects. In a model referred to as 'Form and Flow' (Bray *et al.*, 2015), an attempt was made to conceptually separate the material of the object from its form. The form of the object is an instantiation at a particular point in time – it might be an axe or a cauldron at one particular time, but then, along with other scrap and fresh metal, could be recycled into a bell. The form has changed, but there is some continuity in the life of the material. Under this model, the concept of provenance changes from one in which there is an assumed one-to-one relationship between object and source, to one in which the characteristics of the metal flow (chemical and isotopic) are affected by a number of factors, *one of which* is the source of the metal, but other influences can include the admixture of metal from other sources, or the reintroduction of metal into the flow by recycling. This can be seen as a flowing river, having a source consisting of one or more ore sources, but with different materials being introduced along flow. By monitoring the changes in composition over time, the biography of the *metal flow* can be defined. In the simplest case, where the metal has a single source and there are no further additions, this reduces to the conventional provenance postulate, but in general it is expected to be more complicated than that.

Although this conceptualization might have relevance for copper circulation, and probably by extension to gold and silver, and possibly even for glass, it is difficult to articulate a parallel model for other materials. Here we fall back on a long-term observation – despite all of the obstacles to successful provenance studies articulated in Section 6, there are many situations in which the results are thought to be 'correct'. Does this mean that the objections are irrelevant, perhaps peripheral at best, or is there some other factor at work? The key difference is that archaeology is not geology. Geological factors are, of course, significant – clay has particular properties in particular locations, and ditto metal ores, glassmaking sands, and so on. But these properties are then manipulated by human intervention – clays are processed and mixed, ores are selected and blended, and sands are selected and purified. For example, the large-scale Roman *terra sigillata* factories in Gaul (modern France) have been shown to have produced consistent body compositions over many decades (e.g., at Lezoux: Argyropoulos, 1995). This suggests careful selection and blending of clays and other resources to provide a body with consistent composition having the required physical properties – stiff enough to be moulded, sufficiently calcareous to fire to a glossy red surface, and so on. On an even larger scale, the many billions of pieces of porcelain produced at Jingdezhen, Jiangxi Province, China, for over 1,000 years have been shown to have consistent chemical compositions – there are variations according to quality, vessel size and shape, and some evolution over time (Pollard and Wood, 1986), but the over-riding message is that the people responsible for making the potting clay from the raw materials at Jingdezhen (for this was a separate profession) were exerting considerable control over the selection of the raw materials before the clay was passed to the potters. A similar story emerged in Yunnan in the 19th century with respect to the selection of copper ores for smelting, as revealed by Wu Qujin.

From a provenance perspective, therefore, the obvious differences between archaeology and geology are the interventions made by humans in the steps between the extraction of the raw materials and the production of the finished products, as well as those affecting the life and discard of the objects. In large-scale operations, we are dealing not just with the interventions of a few individuals, but with the sequential activities of a large and complex social organization. In modern terminology, what we are witnessing is the extensive application of 'quality control' over the raw materials of antiquity, exercising huge selective pressures on the exploitation of the available 'resource-scape'.

Where does this leave scientific provenance studies in archaeology – the endeavour embraced so enthusiastically nearly 100 years ago, and which has provided one of the major applications of chemical analysis to archaeology? It is safe to say that for many studies of lithics and obsidian, the existing methodology is and continues to be perfectly satisfactory. The general lack of high temperature processing, and the inability to recycle apart from obvious physical reduction or repurposing, makes it an ideal material. Moving to metals and glass, the situation is less clear. There will undoubtedly be some cases where the traditional model of provenance works well. An example might be the high-status bronze vessels produced for the Royal family during the Shang dynasty in Bronze Age China (c. 1200 BCE). As far as we can tell, these objects did not contain recycled metal, and the raw material supply chain would most likely have been highly controlled, selecting only the finest quality materials (Liu *et al.*, 2020). In such cases we might optimistically expect that a definitive statement can be given about the sources of the raw materials (although the exact sources still remain elusive!). More generally, however, we must expect varying degrees of uncertainty. Despite the many suggestions made to date, it is

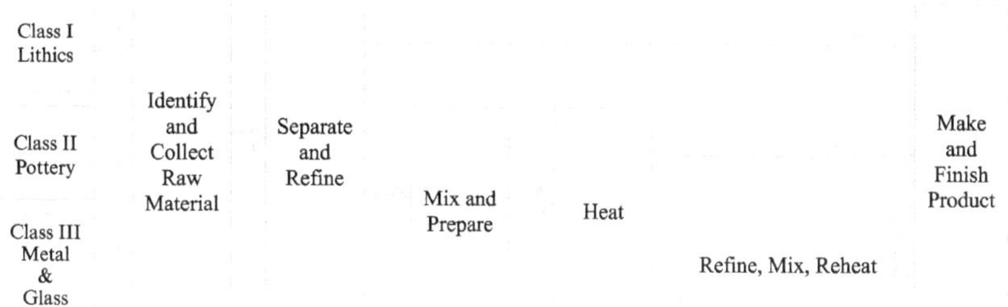

Figure 8 Schematic classification of materials selection and processing. Adapted from Franklin (1983), with the addition of glass to Class III.

still difficult to determine the degree of recycling in any particular object, or even in assemblages of objects.

In 1983, Ursula Martius Franklin (1921–2016) published a schematic diagram showing the selection and manufacturing processes for three classes of materials (Figure 8). Class I is stone ('in which human intervention consists of careful choice of naturally available materials'). Her Class II is 'the naturally occurring constituents – clay, water, and temper – must be selected, prepared, and mixed in proper proportions. From this new composite raw material the object is shaped, . . . heated to more or less elevated temperatures, producing a new material'. Class III (metals) require a two-part operation, one in which the raw material is extracted from its ore, followed by further processes in which the raw metal is refined, mixed (alloyed, possibly with recycled material), and further heated and then converted (cast or worked) into a finished product. In Figure 8, we have added glass to Class III, since glass is often produced at a primary centre, and then coloured and shaped at a secondary centre (see Section 6.3). The significance here for these three classes of material is that it also conveniently, if somewhat simplistically, reflects their suitability for provenance studies – Class I is very suitable, with a good prospect of provenancing to geological source; Class II is suitable for provenance to match, but less likely to be provenanced to source; Class III is potentially too complex to give provenance to source in many cases, but can give provenance to match, although even this is limited by alloying and recycling.

For the more complex (Class II and III) materials, an important line of enquiry lies in the combination of a detailed materials science-based study of the individual steps in the manufacturing process (via raw materials, manufacturing debris, semi-finished products, and so on, if available) combined with targeted provenance studies at each stage. It is clearly easier to study the provenance of actual raw materials recovered from an archaeological excavation of a production site than it is to infer the provenance from the finished or partially processed material; equally, it is probably more fruitful to provenance copper before it is fully refined, or alloyed with other metals. In other words, if the material is available, it is preferable not to attempt to decipher the complex origins of the raw materials from the finished object, but to dissect the process into its component parts. This offers the possibility not only of better understanding the production process but also of unravelling the sources of the different components added at different stages of production.

As always, however, another approach is to change the question. Rather than asking about the provenance of a set of objects, in line with the arguments developed, it might be more fruitful to consider the same data as evidence for the degree of quality assurance exerted on the raw materials. This is perhaps the same as saying that it is easier to resolve the question of 'provenance-to-match' than it is to ask the question of 'provenance-to-source'. Implicitly, it is accepting the notion that quality assurance of raw materials dominates the manufacturing process, and makes it easier to match, for example, unknown *terra sigillata* with known kiln assemblages than it is to identify the actual geological source of the clay. But it is worth thinking beyond these practicalities. The fact that such 'provenance-to-match' studies can be successful indicates that the practices of human control over the selection and processing of raw materials can be studied directly by looking at the variability within the chemical and isotopic data, and also by documenting changes in these factors. Essentially, we are looking at deliberate, repetitive, and consistent human actions manipulating the materials selected from the available 'resource-scape', both locally and occasionally over longer distances. As long ago as 2003, Buxeda and Kilikoglou pointed out that measurements of total variation in ceramic datasets estimated from log-ratio transformations provided an important indicator of 'technologically induced variability, and to the occurrence of alteration and contamination processes', thus providing a tool for such studies (Buxeda and Kilikoglou, 2003: 197). The theme that the (largely ignored) dispersion of chemical data, as opposed to the simple average values, contained important information was further developed by Michelaki and Hancock (2011).

The idea that making pots was a direct reflection of human selection within the landscape – itself not a new idea – was elegantly demonstrated by Michelaki *et al.* (2015). They were considering ceramics from two small Neolithic communities in southern Calabria, Italy, and proposed that these ceramics could be regarded as 'congealed taskscapes' – physical manifestations of the multiple interactions required to construct a pot between people, materials, and landscapes. From a consideration of the different clay resources in the local landscape (4 km radius), and using a combination of X-ray diffraction, optical microscopy, and instrumental NAA, they reconstructed the sources that the potters used, and therefore where they went in the landscape to get their raw materials. Almost incidentally, this also highlighted where they did not go. This revealed a preference for inland resources rather than coastal regions – possibly predicated on the physical properties of the clays, but also potentially related to other perceptions of the suitability of the landscape.

This, and several other examples, shows that chemical analysis within archaeology can reveal many other aspects of past human behaviour, beyond the simple question of 'where does the raw material for this object come from'. The principal requirement is a well-formulated question. Given that archaeology is ultimately about reconstructing human behaviour in the past, this suggests that a broader interpretation of provenance studies, incorporating the study of selective human interventions within the resource-scape, and the complexity of material production processes can actually be far more informative than the question first envisaged in the original concept of provenance.

References

Anon., Early mining and metallurgy group. *Man* **46**, 99 (1946).

Argyropoulos, V., A characterization of the compositional variations of Roman Samian pottery manufactured at the Lezoux production centre. *Archaeometry* **37**, 271–285 (1995).

Asaro, F. and Adan-Bayewitz, D., The history of the Lawrence Berkeley National Laboratory instrumental neutron activation analysis programme for archaeological and geological materials. *Archaeometry* **49**, 201–214 (2007).

Aspinall, A. and Feather, S. W., Neutron activation analysis of prehistoric flint mine products. *Archaeometry* **14**, 41–53 (1972).

Aspinall, A., Warren, S. E., Crummett, J. G., and Newton, R. G., Neutron activation analysis of faience beads. *Archaeometry* **14**, 27–40 (1972).

Aston, F. W., The constitution of atmospheric neon. *Philosophical Magazine* **39** (232), 449–455 (1920a).

Aston, F. W., The mass-spectra of chemical elements. *Philosophical Magazine* **39**(233), 611–625 (1920b).

Aston, F. W., The mass-spectra of chemical elements – Part VI. Accelerated anode rays continued. *Philosophical Magazine* **49**(294), 1191–1201 (1925).

Bagley, R. W., *Shang Ritual Bronzes in the Arthur M. Sackler Collections*. Arthur M. Sackler Foundation, Washington, DC (1987).

Baudouin, M., Procédé pour la détermination des minéraux constituent les haches préhistoriques métalliques: emploi de l'analyse spectrale. *Comptes Rendus Hebdomadaires des Seances de l'Academie des Sciences* **173**, 862–863 (1921).

Beck, H. C. and Stone, J. F. S., *Faience Beads of the British Bronze Age*. Society of Antiquaries, Oxford (1936).

Bentley, M., Gilmour, B., and Pollard, A. M., 'The sword that was broken . . . .': The detection of recycled iron in the archaeological record. *Archaeometry* **65**, 1260–1274 (2023).

Bergman, T. O., Disquisitio chemica de terra gemmarum. *Nova Acta Regiae Societatis Scientiarum Upsaliensis* **III**, 137–170 (1777).

Bergman, T. O., *Dissertatio Chemica de Analysi Ferri*. Edmann, Uppsala (1781).

Bidegaray, A. -I. and Pollard, A. M., Tesserae recycling in the production of medieval blue window glass. *Archaeometry* **60**, 784–796 (2018).

Bieber, A. M. Jr., Brooks, D. W., Harbottle, G., and Sayre, E. V., Application of multivariate techniques to analytical data on Aegean ceramics. *Archaeometry* **18**, 59–74 (1976).

Biek, L., The examination of some copper ores: A report of the ancient mining and metallurgy committee. *Man* **57**, 72–76 (1957).

Biron, I. and Chopinet, M.-H., Colouring, decolouring and opacifying glass. In Janssens, K. (ed.), *Modern Methods for Analysing Archaeological and Historical Glass*, pp. 49–66. Wiley, London (2012).

Bishop, R. L., Five decades of Maya Fine Orange ceramic investigation by INAA. In van Zelst, L. (ed.), *Patterns and Process: A Festschrift in Honor of Dr. Edward V. Sayre*, pp. 80–91. Smithsonian Center for Materials Research and Education. Suitland, Maryland (2003).

Bishop, R. L., Instrumental approaches to understanding Mesoamerican economy: Elusive promises. *Ancient Mesoamerica* **25**(1), 251–269 (2014).

Boulanger, M., Recycling data: Working with published and unpublished ceramic compositional data. In Hunt, A. (ed.), *Oxford Handbook of Archaeological Ceramic Analysis*, pp. 73–84. Oxford University Press, Oxford (2017).

Boulanger, M. T., Digitization of the Lawrence Berkeley Laboratory archaeometric archives: Status update and availability announcement. *Society for Archaeological Sciences Bulletin* **35**(2), 4–7 (2012).

Bray, P., Cuénod, A., Gosden, C., *et al.*, Form and flow: The 'karmic cycle' of copper. *Journal of Archaeological Science* **56**, 202–209 (2015).

Brems, D., Ganio, M., Latruwe, K., *et al.*, Isotopes on the beach, part 2: Neodymium isotopic analysis for the provenancing of Roman glass-making. *Archaeometry* **55**, 449–464 (2013).

Briard, J. and Giot, P.-R., Analyses d'objets métalliques du Chalcolithique, de l'Age du Bronze Ancien et du Bronze Moyen de Bretagne. *L'Anthropologie* **LX**, 495–500 (1956).

Briard, J. and Maréchal, J.-R., Étude technique d'objets métalliques du Chalcolithique et de l'Age du Bronze de Bretagne. *Bulletin de la Société préhistorique de France* **55**, 422–430 (1958).

Brill, R. H., Lead and oxygen isotopes in ancient objects. In Allibone, T. E. (ed.), *The Impact of the Natural Sciences on Archaeology: A Joint Symposium of the Royal Society and the British Academy*, pp. 143–164. The British Academy, London (1970).

Brill, R. H. and Wampler, J. M., Isotope ratios in archaeological objects of lead. In Young, W. J. (ed.), *Application of Science in the Examination of Works of Art: Proceedings of the Seminar: September 7–16, 1965*, pp. 155–166. Museum of Fine Arts, Boston (1967a).

Brill, R. H. and Wampler, J. M., Isotope studies of ancient lead. *American Journal of Archaeology* **71**, 63–77 (1967b).

Brongniart, A., M. Alexandre Brongniart's new work on the history of the art of pottery and of vitrification. *American Journal of Science and Arts* **31**(1), 134–137 (1837).

Brongniart, A., *Traité des Arts Céramiques ou des Poteries Considerérées dans Leur Histoire, Leur Practique et Leur Théorie*. Béchet Jeune, Paris (1844).

Buxeda i Garrigós, J. and Kilikoglou, V., Total variation as a measure of variability in chemical data sets. In van Zelst, L. (ed.), *Patterns and Process: A Festschrift in Honor of Dr. E.V. Sayre*, pp. 185–198. Suitland press, Washington, DC (2003).

Caley, E. R., *The Composition of Ancient Greek Bronze Coins*. American Philosophical Society, Memoirs, Vol. 11, Philadelphia (1939).

Caley, E. R., Klaproth as a pioneer in the chemical investigation of antiquities. *Journal of Chemical Education* **26**, 242–247, 268 (1949).

Caley, E. R., *Analyses of Ancient Glasses 1790–1937: A Comprehensive and Critical Survey*. Corning Museum of Glass, New York (1962).

Caley, E. R., *Analysis of Ancient Metals*. Pergamon Press, Oxford (1964).

Caley, E. R., Chang, I. S. M., and Woods, N. P., Gravimetric and spectrographic analysis of some ancient Chinese copper alloys. *Ars Orientalis* **11**, 183–193 (1979).

Camden, W., *Britannia, sive florentissimorum regnorum Angliæ, Scotiæ, Hiberniæ and Insularum adjacentium ex intima antiquitate chorographica descriptio*. Radulph, London (1586). (First English translation 1610).

Catling, H. W. and Jones, R. E., A reinvestigation of the provenance of the inscribed stirrup jars found at Thebes. *Archaeometry* **19**, 137–146 (1977).

Catling, H. W. and Millett, A., A study in the composition patterns of Mycenaean pictorial pottery from Cyprus. *Annual of the British School at Athens* **60**, 212–224 (1965a).

Catling, H. W. and Millett, A., A study of the inscribed stirrup-jars from Thebes. *Archaeometry* **8**, 5–83 (1965b).

Catling, H. W. and Millett, A., Composition and provenance: A challenge. *Archaeometry* **9**, 92–97 (1966).

Catling, H. W. and Millett, A., Theban stirrup-jars: Questions and answers. *Archaeometry* **11**, 3–20 (1969).

Catling, H. W., Blin-Stoyle, A. E., and Richards, E. E., Spectrographic analysis of Mycenaean and Minoan pottery. *Archaeometry* **4**, 31–38 (1961).

Catling, H. W., Richards, E. E., and Blin-Stoyle, A. E., Correlations between composition and provenance of Mycenaean and Minoan pottery. *Annual of the British School at Athens* **58**, 94–115 (1963).

Chernykh, E. N. (Черных, Е. Н.), История древнейшей металлургии Восточной Европы *Istorii͡a drevneĭsheĭ metallurgii Vostochnoĭ Evropy*

(History of Ancient Metallurgy in Eastern Europe). Материалы и иселования по археологии СССР (Materialy i isselovanija po arkheologii) SSR **132**, Nauka, Moskva (1966).

Chernykh, E. N. (Черных, Е. Н.), Древнейшая металлургия Урала и Поволжья Drevneĭshaia͡ metallurgiia͡ Urala i Povolzhʹia͡ [*Ancient Metallurgy of the Urals and Volga Region*]. Materialy i issledovaniia͡ po arkheologii SSSR 172, Nauka, Moskva (1970).

Chernykh, E. N., *Ancient Metallurgy in the USSR: The Early Metal Age*. Cambridge University Press, Cambridge (1992).

Coghlan, H. H., Ancient Mining and Metallurgy Committee. *Man* **49**, 43 (1949).

Craig, H. and Craig, V., Greek marbles: Determination of provenance by isotopic analysis. *Science* **176**(4033), 401–403 (1972).

Dalton, J., *A New System of Chemical Philosophy*. Russell & Allen, Manchester (1808, 1827). (2 vols.).

Damour, A., Sur la composition des haches en pierre trouvées dans les monuments celtiques et chez les tribus sauvages. *Comptes Rendues Hebdomadaires des Séances de l'Académie des Sciences* **61**, 313–321, 357–368 (1865).

Degryse, P., Isotope-ratio techniques in glass studies. In Janssens, K. (ed.), *Modern Methods for Analysing Archaeological and Historical Glass 1*, pp. 235–245. Wiley, Chichester (2013).

Degryse, P. (ed.), *Glass Making in the Greco-Roman World: Results of the ARCHGLASS Project*. Studies in Archaeological Sciences 4. Leuven University Press, Leuven (2014).

Degryse, P., Schneider, J., Haack, U., *et al.*, Evidence for glass 'recycling' using Pb and Sr isotopic ratios and Sr-mixing lines: The case of early Byzantine Sagalassos. *Journal of Archaeological Science* **33**, 494–501 (2006).

Degryse, P., Henderson, J., and Hodgins, G. (eds.), *Isotopes in Vitreous Materials*. Leuven University Press, Leuven (2009).

Desch, C. H., Sumerian Copper. Report of Committee appointed to report on the probable source of the supply of copper used by the Sumerians. Report on the Metallurgical Examination of Specimens for the Sumerian Committee of the British Association. *Report of the British Association for the Advancement of Science 96th Meeting*, Glasgow 1928, pp. 437–441 (1929).

Devulder, V., Degryse, P., and Vanhaecke, F., Development of a novel method for unraveling the origin of natron flux used in Roman glass production based on B isotopic analysis via multicollector inductively coupled plasma mass spectrometry. *Analytical Chemistry* **85**, 12077–12084 (2013).

Devulder, V., Vanhaecke, F., Shortland, A., *et al.*, Boron isotopic composition as a provenance indicator for the flux raw material in Roman natron glass. *Journal of Archaeological Science* **46**, 107–113 (2014).

Devulder, V., Gerdes, A., Vanhaecke, F., and Degryse, P., Validation of the determination of the B isotopic composition in Roman glasses with laser ablation multi-collector inductively coupled plasma-mass spectrometry. *Spectrochimica Acta Part B: Atomic Spectroscopy* **105**, 116–120 (2015).

Dixon, J. E., Cann, J. R., and Renfrew, C., Obsidian and the origins of trade. *Scientific American* **218**(3), 38–46 (1968).

Dizé, M. J. J., Analyse du cuivre, avec lequel les Anciens fabriquoient leurs Médailles, les Instruments tranchans. *Observations sur la Physique, sur l'Histoire Naturelle et sur les Arts* **36**, 272–276 (1790).

Dostal, J. and Chatterjee, A. K., Contrasting behaviour of Nb/Ta and Zr/Hf ratios in a peraluminous granitic pluton (Nova Scotia, Canada). *Chemical Geology* **163**(1–4), 207–218 (2000).

Duckworth, C. N. and Wilson, A. (eds.), *Recycling and Reuse in the Roman Economy*. Oxford University Press, Oxford (2020).

Dunnell, R. C., Why archaeologists don't care about archaeometry. *Archaeomaterials* **7**(1), 161–165 (1993).

Elliot Smith, Sir G., *The Ancient Egyptians and Their Influence upon the Civilization of Europe*. Harper & Brother, London (1911).

Elliot Smith, Sir G., *The Migrations of Early Cultures: A Study of the Significance of the Geographical Distribution of the Practice of Mummification as Evidence of the Migration of Peoples and the Spread of Certain Customs and Beliefs*. Manchester University Press, Manchester (1915).

Elliot Smith, Sir G., *The Influence of Ancient Egyptian Civilization in the East and in America*. Manchester University Press, Manchester (1916).

Elliot Smith, Sir G., *The Diffusion of Culture*. Watts, London (1933).

Emeleus, V. M., The technique of neutron activation as applied to trace element determination in pottery and coins. *Archaeometry* **1**, 6–15 (1958).

Emeleus, V. M., Studies of ancient ceramic objects by means of neutron bombardment and emission spectroscopy. In Young, W. J. (ed.), *Application of Science in Examination of Works of Art: Proceedings of Seminar, September 15–18*, pp. 153–160. Museum of Fine Arts, Boston (1959).

Emeleus, V. M., Neutron activation analysis of Samian ware sherds. *Archaeometry* **3**, 6–24 (1960).

Emeleus, V. M. and Simpson, G., Neutron activation analysis of ancient Roman potsherds. *Nature* **185**, 196 (1960).

Farnsworth, M. and Ritchie, P. D., Spectrographic studies on ancient glass: Egyptian glass, mainly of the Eighteenth Dynasty, with special reference to its cobalt content. *Technical Studies in the Field of the Fine Arts* **6**(3), 155–168 (1937–1938).

Faure, G., *Principles of Isotope Geology*. Wiley, New York (1986). (2nd ed.).

Fleming, S. J., *Roman Glass; Reflections on Cultural Change*. University of Pennsylvania Museum of Archaeology and Anthropology, Philadelphia (1999).

Foster, H. E., and Jackson, C. M., The composition of Late Romano-British colourless vessel glass: Glass production and consumption. *Journal of Archaeological Science* **37**, 3068–3080 (2010).

Foy, D., Vichy, M., and Picon, M., Les matières premières du verre et la question des produits semi-finis: Antiquité et Moyen Age. In Pétrequin, P., Fluzin, P., Thiriot, J. and Benoit P., (eds.), *Arts du feu et productions artisanales, XXe Rencontres internationales d'Archéologie et d'Histoire d'Antibes, 21–23 octobre 1999*, pp. 419–433. APDCA, Antibes (2000).

Franklin, U. M., The beginnings of metallurgy in China: A comparative approach. In Kuwayama, G. (ed.), *The Great Bronze Age of China: A Symposium*, pp. 94–99. Los Angeles County Museum of Art, Los Angeles (1983).

Freestone, I. and Gaimster, D. R. M. (eds.), *Pottery in the Making: World Ceramic Traditions*. British Museum, London (1997).

Freestone, I. C., Leslie, K. A., Thirlwall, M., and Gorin-Rosen, Y., Strontium isotopes in the investigation of early glass production: Byzantine and early Islamic glass from the Near East. *Archaeometry* **45**, 19–32 (2003).

Frison, G. C., Wright, G. A., Griffin, J. B., and Gordus, A. A., Neutron activation analysis of obsidian: An example of its relevance to northwestern plains archaeology *Plains Anthropologist* **13**(41), 209–217 (1968).

Gale, N. H., Mediterranean obsidian source characterization by strontium isotope analysis. *Archaeometry* **23**, 41–51 (1981).

Gale, N. H., Copper oxhide ingots: Their origin and their place in the Bronze Age Metals Trade in the Mediterranean. In Gale, N. H. (ed.), *Science and Archaeology: Bronze Age Trade in the Mediterranean*, pp. 197–239. Studies in Mediterranean Archaeology XC. P. Åstroms Förlag, Goteborg (1991).

Gale, N. H. and Stos-Gale, Z., Lead and silver in the ancient Aegean. *Scientific American* **244**, 176–193 (1981a).

Gale, N. H. and Stos-Gale, Z. A., Cycladic lead and silver metallurgy. *Annual of the British School at Athens* **76**, 169–224 (1981b).

Gale, N. H. and Stos-Gale, Z. A., Bronze Age copper sources in the Mediterranean: A new approach. *Science* **216**, 11–19 (1982).

Gale, N. H. and Stos-Gale, Z. A., Lead isotope studies in the Aegean – the British Academy Project. In Pollard, A. M. (ed.), *Advances in Archaeological*

Science, pp. 63–108. Proceedings of the British Academy 77, British Academy, London (1992).

Giot, P.-R., Bourhis, J., and Briard, J., *Analyses spectrographiques d'objets préhistoriques et antiques*. Premiere serie. Travaux du Laboratoire d'anthropologie prehistorique, 1964–1965. Laboratoire d'anthropologie préhistorique, Faculté des sciences, Rennes (1966, 1970, 1975, 1979).

Glascock, M. D. and Macdonald, B. L., Multivariate analysis in archaeology. In Pollard, A. M., Armitage, R. A., and Makarewicz, C. (eds.), *Handbook of Archaeological Sciences*, pp. 1183–1192. Wiley, Chichester (2023).

Glascock, M. D. and Neff, H., Neutron activation analysis and provenance research in archaeology. *Measurement Science and Technology* **14**, 1516–1526 (2003).

Göbel, F., *Ueber den Einfluss der Chemie auf die Ermittelung der Völker der Vorzeit oder Resultate der chemischen Untersuchung metallischer Alterthümer insbesondere der in den Ostseegouvernements vorkommenden, Behufs der Ermittelung der Völker, van welchen sie abstammen*. Ferdinand Enke, Erlangen (1842).

Gordus, A. A., Wright, G. A., and Griffin, J. B., Obsidian sources characterized by neutron-activation analysis. *Science* **161**(3839), 382–384 (1968).

Granger, F., *Vitruvius Pollio on Architecture*. Heinemann, London (1931–1934).

Green, G. A., *Gold Coinage in the Roman World: Function and Production*. PhD thesis, University of Warwick (2020).

Greenaway, F., The early development of analytical chemistry. *Endeavour* **21**, 91–97 (1962).

Greenaway, F., The historical continuity of the tradition of assaying. In *Proceedings of the Tenth International Congress of the History of Science: Ithaca 26 VIII – 2 IX 1962, Part 2*, pp. 819–823. Hermann, Paris (1964).

Grögler, N., Geiss, J., Grünefelder, M., and Houtermans, F. G., Isotopenuntersuchungen zur Bestimmung der Herkunft romischer Bleirohre und Bleibarren. *Zeitschrift für Naturforschung* **21**, 1167–1172 (1966).

Hahn-Weinheimer, P., Ueber spektrochemische Untersuchungen an römischen Fenstergläsern. *Glastechnische Berichte* **27**, 459–464 (1954).

Harbottle, G., Chemical characterization in archaeology. In Ericson, J. E. and Earle, T. K. (eds.), *Contexts for Prehistoric Exchange*, pp. 13–51. Academic Press, New York (1982).

Harbottle, G. and Holmes, L., The history of the Brookhaven National Laboratory project in archaeological chemistry, and applying nuclear methods to the fine arts. *Archaeometry* **49**, 185–199 (2007).

Harding, A. and Warren, S. E., Early Bronze Age faience beads from Central Europe. *Antiquity* **47**, 64–66 (1973).

Hawthorne, J. G. and Smith, C. S., *On Divers Arts – the treatise of Theophilus*. Chicago University Press, Chicago (1963).

Henderson, P., *Rare Earth Element Geochemistry*. Elsevier, Oxford (1984).

Hodson, F. R., Searching for structure within multivariate archaeological data. *World Archaeology* **1**, 90–105 (1969).

Hofmann, K. B., Über die schmelzfarben von Tell el Jehüdije. *Zeitschrift für ägyptische Sprache und Alterthumskunde* **XXIII**, 62–68 (1885).

Holmyard, E. J., *The Works of Geber Englished by Richard Russell, 1678*. Dent, London (1928).

Hopkins, O., *The Museum: From Its Origins to the 21st Century*. Frances Lincoln, London (2021).

Hughes, M. J. and Oddy, W. A., A reappraisal of the specific gravity method for the analysis of gold alloys. *Archaeometry* **12**, 1–11 (1970).

Hunt, A., On the origin of ceramics: Moving toward a common understanding on provenance. *Archaeological Review from Cambridge* **27**(1), 85–97 (2012).

Hunt, A. (ed.), *The Oxford Handbook of Archaeological Ceramic Analysis*. Oxford University Press, Oxford (2017).

Jackson, C. M., Cool, H. E. M., and Wager, E. C. W., The manufacture of glass in Roman York. *Journal of Glass Studies* **40**, 55–61 (1998).

Jones, R., *Greek and Cypriot Pottery: A Review of Scientific Studies*. British School at Athens, Athens (1986).

Junghans, S., Sangmeister, E., and Schröder, M., *Metallanalysen kupferzeitlichen mid frühbronzezeitlichen Bodenfunde aus Europa*. Studien zu den Anfangen der Metallurgie 1. Gebr. Mann, Berlin (1960).

Junghans, S., Sangmeister, E., and Schröder, M., *Kupfer und Bronze in der frühen Metallzeit Europas. Studien zu den Anfängen der Metallurgie*. Studien zu den Anfangen der Metallurgie 2, vols. 1–3, Gebr. Mann, Berlin (1968).

Junghans, S., Sangmeister, E., and Schröder, M., *Kupfer und Bronze in der frühen Metallzeit Europas: Katalog der Analysen Nr. 10041–22000 (mit Nachuntersuchungen der Analysen Nr. 1–10400)*. Studien zu den Anfängen der Metallurgie 2.4. Gebr. Mann, Berlin (1974).

Kirchoff, G. and Bunsen, R., Chemische analyse durch spectralbeobachtungen. *Annalen der Physik und Chemie* **CX**, 161–189 (1860).

Klaproth, M. H., Mémoire de numismatique docimastique. *Mémoires de l'Academie Royale des Sciences et Belles-Lettres depuis l'avénement de Fréderic Guillaume II au Trône. (Classe de Philosophie Expérimentale)* **45**, 97–113 (1792/3).

Klaproth, M. H., Sur quelques vitrifications antiques. *Mémoires de l'Académie Royale des Sciences et Belles-Lettres: Classe de Philosophie Expérimentale* **49**, 3–16 (1798).

Knapp, A. B. and Cherry, J. F., *Provenience Studies and Bronze Age Cyprus: Production, Exchange and Politico-Economic Change*. Prehistory Press, Maddison (1994).

Kohl, P. L., *The Making of Bronze Age Eurasia*. Cambridge University Press, Cambridge (2007).

Krause, R., *Studien zur kupfer- und frühbronzezeitlichen Metallurgie zwischen Karpatenbecken und ostsee*. Vorgeschichtliche Forschungen 24, Marie Leidorf, Rahden (2003).

Krause, R. and Pernicka, E., SMAP – The Stuttgart Metal Analysis Project. *Archaologisches Nachrichtenblatt* **3**, 274–291 (1996).

Legg, R. and Fowles, J. (eds.), *Monumenta Britannica, or, A Miscellany of British Antiquities* (Aubrey, J.). Dorset, Sherborne (1980). (2 vols.).

Levey, M., *Chemistry and Chemical Technology in Ancient Mesopotamia*. Elsevier, Amsterdam (1959).

Liritzis, I. and Laskaris, N., Advances in obsidian hydration dating by secondary ion mass spectrometry: World examples. *Nuclear Instruments and Methods in Physics Research Section B* **267**(1), 144–150 (2009).

Liu, R., Bray, P., Pollard, A. M., and Hommel, P., Chemical analysis of ancient Chinese Bronzes: past, present and future. *Archaeological Research in Asia* **3**, 1–8 (2015).

Liu, R., Pollard, A.M., Cao, Q., *et al.*, Social hierarchy and the choice of metal recycling at Anyang, the last capital of Bronze Age Shang China. *Scientific Reports* **10**, 18794 (2020).

Lobo, L., Devulder, V., Degryse, P., and Vanhaecke, F., Investigation of natural isotopic variation of Sb in stibnite ores via multi-collector ICP-mass spectrometry – perspectives for Sb isotopic analysis of Roman glass. *Journal of Analytical Atomic Spectrometry* **27**, 1304–1310 (2012).

Lobo, L., Degryse, P., Shortland, A., and Vanhaecke, F., Isotopic analysis of antimony using multi-collector ICP-mass spectrometry for provenance determination of Roman glass. *Journal of Analytical Atomic Spectrometry* **28**, 1213–1219 (2013).

Lobo, L., Degryse, P., Shortland, A., Eremin, K., and Vanhaecke, F., Copper and antimony isotopic analysis via multi-collector ICP-mass spectrometry for provenancing ancient glass. *Journal of Analytical Atomic Spectrometry* **29**, 58–64 (2014).

Lucas, A., *Ancient Egyptian Materials and Industries*. Arnold, London (1926).

Mauss, M., Essai sur le don: Forme et raison de l'échange dans les sociétés archaïques. *L'Année Sociologique* **1**, 30–180 (1923–1924).

Mcarthur, J. T., Inconsistencies in the composition and provenance studies of the inscribed jars found at Thebes. *Archaeometry* **20**, 177–182 (1978).

Michelaki, K. and Hancock, R. G. V., Chemistry versus data dispersion: Is there a better way to assess and interpret archaeometric data? *Archaeometry* **53**(6), 1259–1279 (2011).

Michelaki, K., Braun, G. V., and Hancock, R. G. V., Local clay sources as histories of human – landscape interactions: A ceramic taskscape perspective. *Journal of Archaeological Method and Theory* **22**, 783–827 (2015).

Millet, A. and Catling, H. W., Composition patterns of Minoan and Mycenean pottery: Survey and prospects. *Archaeometry* **10**, 70–77 (1967).

Muhly, J. D., Early Bronze Age tin and the Taurus. *American Journal of Archaeology* **97**, 239–254 (1993).

Neumann, B., Antike Gläser, ihre Zusammensetzung und Färbung. *Zeitschrift für angewandte Chemie* **38**, 776–780, 857–864 (1925); II. **40**, 963–967 (1927); III. Assyrich–babylonische Gläser, **41**, 203–204 (1928); IV. **42**, 835–838 (1929).

Nier, A. O., Variations in the relative abundances of the isotopes of common lead from various sources. *Journal of the American Chemical Society* **60**, 1571–1576 (1938).

Okunev, A. I. (Окунев, А.И.), Поведение некоторых редких и рассеянных элементов в процессах металлургической переработки медных руд и концентратов (*The Behaviour of Some Rare and Trace Elements in the Process of Metallurgical Processing of Copper Ores and Concentrates)*. Nauka, Moscow (1960).

Oldeberg, A., *Metallteknik under Förhistorik Tid*. Harrassowitz, Lund (1942–1943). (2 vols.).

Oldroyd, D. R., Some eighteenth century methods for the chemical analysis of minerals. *Journal of Chemical Education* **50**, 337–340 (1973).

Olin, J. S. and Franklin, A. D. (eds.), *Archaeological Ceramics*. Smithsonian Institution Press, Washington, DC (1982).

Orton, C. and Hughes, M., *Pottery in Archaeology*. Cambridge University Press, Cambridge (2013).

Otto, H. and Witter, W., *Handbuch der ältesten vorgeschichtlichen Metallurgie in Mitteleuropa*. Johann Ambrosius Barth, Leipzig (1952).

Parker Pearson, M., Pollard, J., Richards, C., *et al.*, Megalith quarries for Stonehenge's bluestones. *Antiquity* **93**, 45–62 (2019).

Pernicka, E., A short history of provenance analysis of archaeological metal objects. In Aspes, A. (ed.), *I Bronzi del Garda: Valorizzazione delle Collezioni di Bronzi Preistorici di Uno dei Più Importanti Centri Metallurgici dell'Europa del II Millennio A.C.*, pp. 27–37. Memorie del Museo Civico di Storia Naturale di Verona/Sezione Scienze dell'Uomo. Museo Civico di Storia Naturale, Verona (2011).

Pernicka, E., Provenance determination of archaeological metal objects. In Roberts, B. W. and Thornton, C. P. (eds.), *Archaeometallurgy in Global Perspective*, pp. 239–268. Springer, London (2014).

Pettus, Sir J., *Fleta Minor, or, The Laws of Art and Nature in Knowing, Judging, Assaying, Fining, Refining, and Inlarging the Bodies of Confin'd Metals: In Two Parts. The First Contains Assays of Lazarus Erckern … in v. Books; Originally Written by Him in the Teutonick Language, and Now Translated into English. The Second Contains Essays on Metallick Words, as a Dictionary to Many Pleasing Discoveries*. Dawks, London (1683).

Pittioni, R., *Urzeitlicher Bergbau auf Kupfererz und Spurenanalyse: Beiträge zum Problem der Relation Lagerstätte-Fertigobjekt*. Archiv für ur- und frühgeschichtliche Bergbauforschung, 10. F. Deuticke, Wien (1957).

Pollard, A. M., A critical study of multivariate methods as applied to provenance data. In Aspinall, A. and Warren, S. E. (eds.), *Proceedings of the 22nd Symposium on Archaeometry, University of Bradford, March 30th – April 3rd, 1982*, pp. 56–66. University of Bradford, Bradford (1983).

Pollard, A. M., Letters from China – a history of the origins of the chemical analysis of ceramics. *Ambix* **62**, 50–71 (2015).

Pollard, A. M., The first hundred years of archaeometallurgical chemistry: Pownall (1775) to von Bibra (1869). *Journal of the Historical Metallurgy Society* **49**(1), 37–49 (2016).

Pollard, A. M., Johann Christian Wiegleb and the first published chemical analyses of archaeological bronzes. *Journal of the Historical Metallurgy Society* **21**(1), 48–54 (2018).

Pollard, A. M. and Bray, P. J., A new method for combining lead isotope and lead abundance data to characterise archaeological copper alloys. *Archaeometry* **57**, 996–1008 (2015).

Pollard, A. M. and Gosden, C., *An Archaeological Perspective on the History of Technology*. CUP Elements. Cambridge University Press, Cambridge (2023).

Pollard, A. M. and Wood, N. D., Development of Chinese porcelain technology at Jingdezhen. In Olin, J. S. and Blackman, M. J. (eds.), *Proceedings of the 24th International Archaeometry Symposium*, pp. 105–114. Smithsonian Institution, Washington DC (1986).

Pollard, M., Batt, C., Stern, B., and Young, S. M. M., *Analytical Chemistry in Archaeology*. Cambridge University Press, Cambridge (2007).

Pollard, A. M., Bray, P., Gosden, C., Wilson, A., and Hamerow, H., Characterising copper-based metals in Britain in the first millennium AD: A preliminary quantification of metal flow and recycling. *Antiquity* **89**, 697–713 (2015).

Pollard, A. M., Heron, C., and Armitage, R. A., *Archaeological Chemistry*. Royal Society of Chemistry, Cambridge (2017).

Pollard, A. M., Bray, P., Cuénod, A., *et al.*, *Beyond Provenance: The Interpretation of Chemical and Isotopic Data in Archaeological Bronzes*. Studies in Archaeological Science, University of Leuven Press, Leuven (2018).

Pollard, A. M., Armitage, R. A., and Makarewicz, C. (eds.), *Handbook of Archaeological Sciences*. Wiley, Chichester (2023a).

Pollard, A. M., Ma, Q., Bidegaray, A.-I., and Liu, R., The use of kernel density estimates on chemical and isotopic data in archaeology. In Pollard, A. M., Armitage, R. A., and Makarewicz, C. (eds.), *Handbook of Archaeological Sciences*, pp. 1227–1240. Wiley, Chichester (2023b).

Polyani, K., *The Great Transformation: The Political and Economic Origins of Our Time*. Beacon Press, Boston (1944).

Preuschen, E. and Pittioni, R., *Untersuchungen im Bergbaugebiete Kelchalpe bei Kitzbühel, Tirol: 1. Bericht über die Arbeiten 1931–1936 zur Uregeschichte des Kupferbergwesens in Tirol*. Mitteilungen der Prähistorischen Kommission der Österreichischen Akademie der Wissenschaften **3**, Wien (1937).

Price, T. D. and Burton, J. H., Provenience and provenance. In Price, T. D. and Burton, J. H. (eds.), *An Introduction to Archaeological Chemistry*, pp. 213–242. Springer, New York (2011).

Raison, J., *Les Vases à Inscriptions Peintes de l'Age Mycénien et leur Contexte Archéologique*. Incunabula Graeca, XIX. Centro di Studi Micenei, Universita di Roma, Rome (1968).

Rawson, J., *Western Zhou Ritual Bronzes from the Arthur M. Sackler Collections*. Arthur M. Sackler Foundation, Washington, DC (1990).

Renfrew, C. and Bahn, P., *Archaeology: Theories, Methods and Practice*. Thames and Hudson, London (2020). (8th ed.).

Renfrew, C., Cann, J. R. and Dixon, J. E., Obsidian in the Aegean. *Annual of the British School at Athens* **60**, 225–247 (1965).

Rice, P. M., *Pottery Analysis: A Sourcebook*. University of Chicago Press, Chicago (1987).

Richards, E. E., Spectrographic investigation of some Romano-British mortaria. *Archaeometry* **2**, 23–31 (1959).

Richards, T. W., The composition of Athenian pottery. *American Chemical Journal* **57**, 152–154 (1895).

Riehle, K., Kistler, E., Öhlinger, B., *et al.*, Neutron activation analysis in Mediterranean archaeology: Current applications and future perspectives. *Archaeological and Anthropological Sciences* **15**(3), 25 (2023).

Ritchie, P. D., Spectrographic studies on ancient glass: Chinese glass, from Pre-Han to T'ang times. *Technical Studies in the Field of the Fine Arts* **5**(4), 209–220 (1936–1937).

Roberts, B. W., Thornton, C. P., and Pigott, V. C., Development of metallurgy in Eurasia. *Antiquity* **83**, 1012–1022 (2009).

Sabloff, J., Analyses of fine paste ceramics. In Willey, G. R. (ed.), *Excavations at Seibal, Department of Petan, Guatemala*, pp. 265–343. Memoirs of the Peabody Museum of Archaeology and Ethnology, Vol. 15, Nos. 1 and 2. Harvard University Press, Cambridge, MA (1982).

Sainsbury, V. A., When things stopped travelling: Recycling and the glass industry in Britain from the first to fifth century CE. In Rosenow, D., Phelps, M., Meek, A., and Freestone, I. (eds.), *Things that Travelled: Mediterranean Glass in the First Millennium CE*, pp. 324–345. UCL Press, London (2018).

Sayre, E. V. and Dodson, R. W., Neutron activation study of Mediterranean potsherds. *American Journal of Archaeology* **61**, 35–41 (1957).

Sayre, E. V. and Smith, R. W., Compositional categories of ancient glass. *Science* **133**(3467), 1824–1826 (1961).

Schubert, F. and Schubert, E., Spektralanalytische Untersuchungenvon Hort- und Einzelfunden der Periode BIII. In Mozsolics, A. (ed.), *Bronzefunde des Karpatenbeckens: Depotfundhorizonte von Hajdúsámson und Kosziderpadlás*, pp. 185–223. Akadémiai Kiadó, Budapest (1967).

Seligman, C. G. and Beck, H. C., Far eastern glass: Some western origins. *Bulletin of the Museum of Far Eastern Antiquities* **10**, 1–64 (1938).

Seligman, C. G., Ritchie, P. D., and Beck, H. C., Early Chinese glass from pre-Han to Tang times. *Nature* **138**, 721 (1936).

Sena, Y. C., *Bronze and Stone: The Cult of Antiquity in Song Dynasty China*. University of Washington Press, Seattle (2019).

Shaw, S., *The Chemistry of the Several Natural and Artificial Heterogeneous Compounds Used in Manufacturing Porcelain, Glass, and Pottery*. Lewis and Son, London (1837).

Shepard, A. O., Technology of Pecos pottery. In Kidder, A. V. and Shepard, A. O. (eds.), *The Pottery of Pecos: Papers of the Phillips Academy Southwestern Expedition 2*, pp. 389–587. Yale University Press, New Haven (1936).

Shepard, A. O., *Ceramics for the Archaeologist*. Carnegie Institution of Washington 609, Washington DC (1956).

Shortland, A., *Lapis Lazuli from the Kiln: Glass and Glass Making in the Late Bronze Age*. Leuven University Press, Leuven (2012).

Shortland, A., Rogers, N., and Eremin, K., Trace element discriminants between Egyptian and Mesopotamian Late Bronze Age glasses. *Journal of Archaeological Science* **34**, 781–789 (2007).

Sieveking, G. de G. and Hart, M. B., *The Scientific Study of Flint and Chert*. Cambridge University Press, Cambridge (1986).

Sieveking, G. de G., Craddock, P. T., Hughes, M. J., Bush, P., and Ferguson, J., Characterization of prehistoric flint mine products. *Nature* **228**, 251–254 (1970).

Silvestri, A., Molin, G., and Salviulo, G., The colourless glass of Iulia Felix. *Journal of Archaeological Science* **35**, 331–341 (2008).

Sisco, A. G. and Smith, C. S., *Bergwerk-und Probierbüchlein: A Translation from the German of the Bergbüchlein a Sixteenth-Century Book on Mining Geology*. American Institute of Mining and Metallurgical Engineers, New York (1949).

Sisco, A. G. and Smith, C. S., *Lazarus Ercker's Treatise on Ores and Assaying*. University of Chicago, Chicago (1951).

So, J., *Eastern Zhou Ritual Bronzes in the Arthur M. Sackler Collections*. Arthur M. Sackler Foundation, Washington, DC (1995).

Stone, J. F. S. and Thomas, L. C., The use and distribution of faience in the ancient east and prehistoric Europe, with notes on the spectrochemical analysis of faience. *Proceedings of the Prehistoric Society* **22**, 37–84 (1956).

Stos-Gale, Z. A. and Gale, N. H., The sources of Mycenaean silver and lead. *Journal of Field Archaeology* **9**, 467–485 (1982).

Stukeley, W., *Stonehenge a Temple Restor'd to the British Druids*. Innys and Manby, London (1740).

Thompson, F. C., The early metallurgy of copper and bronze: A report to the Ancient Mining and Metallurgy Committee of the Royal Anthropological Institute. *Man* **58**, 1–7 (1958).

Trigger, B., *A History of Archaeological Thought*. Cambridge University Press, Cambridge (1989).

Tykot, R. H., Non-destructive pXRF on prehistoric obsidian artifacts from the Central Mediterranean. *Applied Sciences* **11**, 7459 (2021).

Vauquelin, L. N., Reflections on the qualities of pottery, with the results of some analyses of earths and of common pottery. *Journal of Natural Philosophy, Chemistry & the Arts* **3**, 262–264 (1800).

Vauquelin, L. N., Réflections sur l'analyse des pierres en general, et résultats de plusiers de ces analyses faites au laboratoire de l'école des mines depuis quelques mois. *Annales de Chimie* **30**, 66–106 (1799).

Velde, B., Glass compositions over several millennia in the Western World. In Janssens, K. (ed.), *Modern Methods for Analysing Archaeological and Historical Glass, Volume I*, pp. 67–78. Wiley, Chichester (2013).

Vogel, H. U., Copper smelting and fuel consumption in Yunnan, eighteenth to nineteenth centuries. In Hirzel, T. and Kim, N. (eds.), *Metals, Moneys and Markets in Early Modern Societies: East Asian and Global Perspectives*, pp. 119–170. Bunka Wenhua Tubingen East Asian Studies 17. LIT Verlag, Berlin (2008).

von Bibra, E. F., *Die Bronzen und Kupferlegirung der alten und ältesten Völker, mit Rücksichtnahme auf jene der Neuzeit*. Ferdinand Enke, Erlangen (1869).

von Engeström, G., Försök på naturlig flos zinci ifrån China (On natural flos zinci from China). *Kungliga Vetenskaps Academiens Handlingar* **36**, 78–85 (1775).

von Engeström, G., Pak-Fong, ein Chinesisches weiss metal. *Der Königlichen Schwedischen Akademie der Wissenschaften neue Abhandlungen, aus der Naturlehre, Haushaltungskunst und Mechanik* **38**, 40–42 (1776).

Walton, M. S., Shortland, A., Kirk, S., and Degryse, P., Evidence for the trade of Mesopotamian and Egyptian glass to Mycenaean Greece. *Journal of Archaeological Science* **36**, 1496–1503 (2009).

Wang, Z. 王宗沐, 江西省大志 Jiang-xi sheng da zhi (*The Great Gazette of Jiang-xi Province*). Chengwen chubanshe 成文出版社 Cheng Wen Press, Taibei 台北 (1597).

Waterbolk, H. T. and Butler, J. J., Comments on the use of metallurgical analysis in prehistoric studies. *Helinium* **V**, 227–251 (1965).

Watson, J. H., *Ancient Trial Plates: A Description of the Ancient Gold and Silver Trial Plates Deposited in the Pyx Stronghold of the Royal Mint*. H.M.S. O, London (1962).

Weigand, P. C., Harbottle, G., and Sayre, E. V., Turquoise sources and source analysis: Mesoamerican and the Southwestern USA. In Earle, T. K. and Ericson, J. E. (eds.), *Exchange Systems in Prehistory*, pp. 15–34. Academic Press, New York (1977).

Wiegleb, J. C., Chemisch Untersuchung einiger künstlichen Metallarten, woraus verschiedene aus dem Altertum herrührende Instrumente versertiget gewesen, welche im vorigen Jahre in einer benachbarten Gegend gefunden worden find. *Acta Academiae Electoralis Moguntinae Scientiarum Utilium, quae Erfurti est*, 50–57 (1777).

Wilson, A. L., The provenance of the inscribed stirrup-jars found at Thebes. *Archaeometry* **18**, 51–58 (1976).

Wilson, L. and Pollard, A. M., The provenance hypothesis. In Brothwell, D. R. and Pollard, A. M. (eds.), *Handbook of Archaeological Sciences*, pp. 507–517. John Wiley and Sons, Chichester (2001).

Wright, G. A., *Obsidian Analyses and Early Trade in the Near East: 7500 to 3500 B.C.* Ph.D. Thesis, Anthropology, History, Archaeology, University of Michigan (1968).

Zhang, W. and Hu, Z., A critical review of isotopic fractionation and interference correction methods for isotope ratio measurements by laser ablation multi-collector inductively coupled plasma mass spectrometry. *Spectrochimica Acta Part B: Atomic Spectroscopy* **171**, 105929 (2020).

Cambridge Elements

Current Archaeological Tools and Techniques

Hans Barnard

Cotsen Institute of Archaeology

Hans Barnard was associate adjunct professor in the Department of Near Eastern Languages and Cultures as well as associate researcher at the Cotsen Insitute of Archaeology, both at the University of California, Los Angeles. He currently works at the Roman site of Industria in northern Italy and previously participated in archaeological projects in Armenia, Chile, Egypt, Ethiopia, Italy, Iceland, Panama, Peru, Sudan, Syria, Tunisia, and Yemen. This is reflected in the seven books and more than 100 articles and chapters to which he contributed.

Willeke Wendrich

Polytechnic University of Turin

Willeke Wendrich is Professor of Cultural Heritage and Digital Humanities at the Politecnico di Torino (Turin, Italy). Until 2023 she was Professor of Egyptian Archaeology and Digital Humanities at the University of California, Los Angeles, and the first holder of the Joan Silsbee Chair in African Cultural Archaeology. Between 2015 and 2023 she was Director of the Cotsen Institute of Archaeology, with which she remains affiliated. She managed archaeological projects in Egypt, Ethiopia, Italy, and Yemen, and is on the board of the International Association of Egyptologists, Museo Egizio (Turin, Italy), the Institute for Field Research, and the online UCLA Encyclopedia of Egyptology.

About the Series

Cambridge University Press and the Cotsen Institute of Archaeology at UCLA collaborate on this series of Elements, which aims to facilitate deployment of specific techniques by archaeologists in the field and in the laboratory. It provides readers with a basic understanding of selected techniques, followed by clear instructions how to implement them, or how to collect samples to be analyzed by a third party, and how to approach interpretation of the results.

Cambridge Elements

Current Archaeological Tools and Techniques

Elements in the Series

Archaeological Mapping and Planning
Hans Barnard

Mobile Landscapes and Their Enduring Places
Bruno David, Jean-Jacques Delannoy and Jessie Birkett-Rees

Cultural Burning
Bruno David, Michael-Shawn Fletcher, Simon Connor, Virginia Ruth Pullin, Jessie Birkett-Rees, Jean-Jacques Delannoy, Michela Mariani, Anthony Romano and S. Yoshi Maezumi

Machine Learning for Archaeological Applications in R
Denisse L. Argote, Pedro A. López-García, Manuel A. Torres-García and Michael C. Thrun

Knowledge Discovery from Archaeological Materials
Pedro A. López-García, Denisse L. Argote, Manuel A. Torres-García and Michael C. Thrun

Worked Bone, Antler, Ivory, and Keratinous Materials
Adam DiBattista

Retrospective and Prospective for Scientific Provenance Studies in Archaeology
A.M. Pollard

A full series listing is available at: www.cambridge.org/EATT

www.ingramcontent.com/pod-product-compliance
Lightning Source LLC
Chambersburg PA
CBHW072333030325
22904CB00008B/389

* 9 7 8 1 0 0 9 5 9 2 2 2 2 *